English Law and the Renaissance

FREDERIC WILLIAM MAITLAND

1901

TABLE OF CONTENTS

DEDICATION
ENGLISH LAW AND THE RENAISSANCE
NOTES

DEDICATION

TO JAMES BRADLEY THAYER, LL.D. PROFESSOR OF LAW AT HARVARD UNIVERSITY.

ENGLISH LAW AND THE RENAISSANCE

Mr Vice-Chancellor and Fellow-Students:

Were we to recall to life the good Sir Robert Rede who endowed lecturers in this university, we might reasonably hope that he would approve and admire the fruit that in these last years has been borne by his liberality. And then, as in private duty or private interest bound, I would have him speak thus: 'Yes, it is marvellous and more than marvellous this triumph of the sciences that my modest rent-charge stimulates you annually to record; nor do I wonder less at what my lecturers have said of humane letters and the fine arts, of the history of all times and of my time, of Erasmus whom I remember, and that age of the Renaissance (as you call it) in which (so you say) I lived. But there is one matter, one science (for such we accounted it) of which they seem to have said little or nothing; and it happens to be a matter, a science, in which I used to take some interest and which I endeavoured to teach. You have not, I hope, forgotten that I was not only an English judge, but, what is more, a reader in English law1.'

Six years ago a great master of history, whose untimely death we are deploring, worked the establishment of the Rede lectures into the picture that he drew for us of The Early Renaissance in England2. He brought Rede's name into contact with the names of Fisher and More. That, no doubt, is the right environment and this pious founder's care for the humanities, for logic and for philosophy natural and moral was a memorable sign of the times. Nevertheless the fact remains that, had it not been for his last will and testament, we should hardly have known Sir Robert except as an English lawyer who throve so well in his profession that he became Chief Justice of the Common Bench. And the rest of the acts of Robert Rede—we might say—and the arguments that he urged and the judgments that he pronounced, are they not written in queer old French

7

in the Year Books of Henry VII and Henry VIII? Those ancient law reports are not a place in which we look for humanism or the spirit of the Renaissance: rather we look there for an amazingly continuous persistence and development of medieval doctrine.

Perhaps we should hardly believe if we were told for the first time that in the reign of James I a man who was the contemporary of Shakespeare and Bacon, a very able man too and a learned, who left his mark deep in English history, said, not by way of paradox but in sober earnest, said repeatedly and advisedly, that a certain thoroughly medieval book written in decadent colonial French was 'the most perfect and absolute work that ever was written in any human science3.' Yet this was what Sir Edward Coke said of a small treatise written by Sir Thomas Littleton, who, though he did not die until 1481, was assuredly no child of the Renaissance.

I know that the names of Coke and Littleton when in conjunction are fearsome names or tiresome, and in common honesty I am bound to say that if you stay here you will be wearied. Still I feel that what is at fault is not my theme. A lecturer worthy of that theme would—I am sure of it—be able to convince you that there is some human interest, and especially an interest for English-speaking mankind, in a question which Coke's words suggest:—How was it and why was it that in an age when old creeds of many kinds were crumbling and all knowledge was being transfigured, in an age which had revolted against its predecessor and was fully conscious of the revolt, one body of doctrine and a body that concerns us all remained so intact that Coke could promulgate this prodigious sentence and challenge the whole world to contradict it4? I have not the power to tell and you to-day have not the time to hear that story as it should be told. A brief outline of what might be said is all that will be possible and more than will be tolerable.

Robert Rede died in January, 1519. Let us remember for a moment where we stand at that date. The Emperor Maximilian also was dying. Henry VIII was reigning in England, Francis I in France, Charles I in Spain, Leo X at Rome. But come we to jurisprudence. Is it beneath the historic muse to notice that young Mr More, the judge's son, had lately lectured at Lincoln's Inn5? Perhaps so. At all events for a while we will speak of more resonant exploits. We could hardly (so I learn at second-hand) fix a better date than that of Rede's death for the second new birth of Roman law. More's friend Erasmus had turned his back on England and was by this time in correspondence with two accomplished jurists, the Italian Andrea Alciato and the German Ulrich Zäsi. They and the French scholar Guillaume Bude were publishing books which mark the beginning of a new era6. Humanism was renovating Roman law. The medieval commentators, the Balduses and Bartoluses, the people whom Hutten and Rabelais7 could deride, were in like case with Peter Lombard, Duns Scotus and other men of the night.

Back to the texts! was the cry, and let the light of literature and history play upon them8. The great Frenchmen who were to do the main part of the work and to make the school of Bourges illustrious were still young or unborn; Cujas was born in 1522; but already the advanced guard was on the march and the flourish of trumpets might be heard9. And then in 1520— well, we know what happened in 1520 at Wittenberg, but perhaps we do not often remember that when the German friar ceremoniously and contumeliously committed to the flames some venerated lawbooks—this, if an event in the history of religion, was also an event in the history of jurisprudence. A current of new life was thrilling through one Corpus Juris10; the other had been sore stricken, and, if it escaped from violent death, might perish yet more miserably of a disease that becomes dangerous at the moment when it is discovered.

A few years afterwards an enlightened young humanist, of high rank and marked ability, a man who might live to be pope of Rome or might live to be king of England, was saying much evil of the sort of law that Rede had administered and taught; was saying that a wise prince would banish this barbaric stuff and receive in its stead the civil law of the Romans. Such, so we learn from one of his friends, was the talk of Reginald Pole, and a little knowledge of what was happening in foreign countries is enough to teach us that such talk deserves attention11.

This was the time when Roman law was driving German law out of Germany or forcing it to conceal itself in humble forms and obscure corners12. If this was the age of the Renaissance and the age of the Reformation, it was also the age of the 'Reception.' I need not say that this Reception—the reception of Roman law—plays a large part in modern versions of German history, and by no means only in such as are written by lawyers. I need not say that it has been judged from many different points of view, that it has been connected by some with political, by others with religious and by yet others with economic changes. Nor need I say that of late years few writers have had a hearty good word for the Reception. We have all of us been nationalists of late. Cosmopolitanism can afford to await its turn13.

Then we observe that not long after Pole had been advocating a Reception, his cousin King Henry, whose word was law supreme in church and state, prohibited the academic study of one great and ancient body of law—the canon law14—and encouraged the study of another—the civil law—by the foundation of professorships at Oxford and Cambridge. We observe also that his choice of a man to fill the chair at Cambridge fell on one who was eminently qualified to represent in his own person that triad of the three R's—Renaissance, Reformation and Reception. We know Professor Thomas Smith as a humanist, an elegant scholar with advanced opinions about the pronunciation of Greek. We know the Reverend Thomas Smith as a decided, if cautious, protestant whose doings are of some interest to those who study the changeful history of ecclesiastical affairs. Then we know Dr Thomas Smith as a doctor in law of the university of Padua, for with praiseworthy zeal when he was appointed professor at Cambridge he journeyed to the fountain-head for his Roman law and his legal degree15. Also he visited those French universities whence a new jurisprudence was beginning to spread. He returned to speak to us in two inaugural lectures of this new jurisprudence: to speak with enthusiasm of Alciatus and Zasius16: to speak hopefully of the future that lay before this conquering science— the future that lay before it in an England fortunately ruled by a pious, wise, learned and munificent Prince. Then in Edward VI's day Thomas Smith as a Master of Requests was doing justice in a court whose procedure was described as being 'altogether according to the process of summary causes in the civil law ' and at that moment this Court of Requests and other courts with a like procedure seemed to have time, reason and popularity upon their side17. Altogether, the Rev. Prof. Dr Sir Thomas Smith, Knt., M.P., Dean of Carlisle, Provost of Eton, Ambassador to the Court of France and Secretary of State to Queen Elizabeth was a man of mark in an age of great events. Had some of those events been other than they were, we might now be saying of him that he played a prominent part in Renaissance, Reformation and Reception, and a part characteristic of that liberal and rational university of which he was professor, public orator and vice-chancellor18.

Some German historians, as you are aware, have tried to find or to fashion links that will in some direct and obvious manner connect the Reformation and the Reception. In one popular version of the tale protestantism finds a congenial ally in the individualism and capitalism of the pagan Digest19. In truth I take it that the story is complex. Many currents and cross-currents were flowing in that turbid age. It so happens that in this country we can connect with the heresiarchal name of Wyclif a proposal for the introduction of English law, as a substitute for Roman law, into the schools of Oxford and Cambridge20. On the other hand, the desire for a practical Reception of the civil law is ascribed to the future cardinal, who in his last days reconciled England for a moment, not with the Rome of the Digest, but with the Rome of the Decretals. And by the way we may notice that when the cardinal was here upon his reconciliatory errand he had for a while as his legal adviser one of the most learned lawyers of that age, the Spaniard Antonio Agustin. But we in England take little notice of this famous man, who, so foreigners assure us now-a-days, began the historical study of the canon law and knew more about the false Isidore than it was comfortable for him to know21. Our Dr Smith was protestant enough; but his Oxford colleague Dr John Story showed zeal in the cremation of protestants, helped Alva (so it is said) to establish the Inquisition in the

Netherlands, was hanged as a traitor at Tyburn in 1571 and beatified as a martyr at Rome in 1886. Blessed John Story was zealous; but his permanent contribution to the jurisprudence of his native land was (so far as I am aware) an early precedent for the imprisonment of a disorderly member by the House of Commons, and a man may be disorderly without being a jurist22. Ulrich Zäsi went part of the way with Luther; but then stayed behind with Erasmus23. He had once compared the work that he was doing for the Corpus Juris with the work that Luther was doing for the Bible24. The great Frenchmen answered the religious question in different ways. One said 'That has nothing to do with the praetor's edict.' His rivals charged him with a triple apostasy25. Three or four of them were stout huguenots, and we must not forget that Calvin and Beza had both been at Bourges and had both studied the civil law. Melanchthon also was a warm admirer of Roman jurisprudence26. It is reported that Elizabeth invited Francis Hotman to Oxford27. He was protestant enough, and fierce enough to exchange letters with a tiger28. He is best known to English law-students as the man who spoke light words of Littleton and thus attracted Coke's thunderbolt29; but if he thought badly of Littleton, he thought badly of Tribonian also, and would have been the last man to preach a Reception. Professor Alberigo Gentili of Oxford, he too was protestant enough and could rail at the canonists by the hour; but then he as an Italian had a bitter feud with the French humanizers, and stood up for the medieval gloss30.

Plainly the story is not simple and we must hurry past it. Still the perplexity of detail should not obscure the broad truth that there was pleasant reading in the Byzantine Code for a king who wished to be monarch in church as well as state: pleasanter reading than could be found in our ancient English law-books. Surely Erastianism is a bad name for the theory that King Henry approved: Marsilianism seems better, but Byzantinism seems best31. A time had come when, medieval spectacles being discarded, men could see with the naked eye what stood in the Code and Novels of Constantinople. In 1558 on the eve of an explosive Reformation 'the Protestants of Scotland,' craving 'remedy against the tyranny of the estate ecclesiastical,' demanded that the controversy should be judged by the New Testament, the ancient fathers 'and the godly approved laws of Justinian the emperor32.' University-bred jurists, even such as came from an oldish school, were very serviceable to King Henry in the days of the great divorce case and the subsequent quarrel with the papacy. Tunstall, Gardiner, Bonner, Sampson and Clerk, to say nothing of the Leghs and Laytons, were doctors of law and took their fees in bishoprics and deaneries33. Certainly they were more conspicuous and probably they were much abler men than those who were sitting in the courts of the common law. With the one exception of Anthony Fitzherbert, the judges of Henry's reign are not prominent in our legal history, and we have little reason for attributing deep knowledge of any sort of law to such chancellors as Audley, Wriothesley and Rich. I doubt our common lawyers easily accommodated themselves to ecclesiastical changes. Some years after Elizabeth's accession the number of barristers who were known to the government as 'papists' was surprisingly large and it included the great Plowden34. But we must go back to our main theme.

A Reception there was not to be, nor dare I say that a Reception was what our Regius Professor or his royal patron desired. As to Smith himself, it is fairly evident that some time afterwards, when he had resigned his chair and was Elizabeth's ambassador at the French court, he was well content to contrast the public law of England with that of 'France, Italy, Spain, Germany and all other countries which' to use his words 'do follow the civil law of the Romans compiled by Justinian into his Pandects and Code35.' The little treatise on the Commonwealth of England which he wrote at Toulouse in 1565—a remarkable feat for he had no English books at hand36—became a classic in the next century, and certainly did not underrate those traditional, medieval, Germanic and parliamentary elements which were still to be found in English life and law under the fifth and last of the Tudors. Nevertheless I think that a well-equipped lecturer might persuade a leisurely audience to perceive that in the second quarter of the sixteenth century the continuity of English legal history was seriously threatened37.

Unquestionably our medieval law was open to humanistic attacks. It was couched partly in bad Latin, partly in worse French. For the business Latin of the middle age there is much to be said. It is a pleasant picture that which we have of Thomas More puzzling the omniscient foreigner by the question 'An averia carucae capta in withernamio sunt irreplegibilia38.' He asked a practical question in the only Latin in which that question could have been asked without distortion. Smith's acute glance saw that withernamium must have something to do with the German wiedernehmen; for among his other pursuits our professor had interested himself in the study of English words39. But this business Latin was a pure and elegant language when compared with what served our lawyers as French. Pole and Smith might well call it barbarous; that it was fast becoming English was its one redeeming feature. You are likely to know what I must not call the classical passage: it comes from the seventeenth century. In all the Epistolae Obscurorum Virorum there is nothing better than the report which tells how one of Sir Robert Rede's successors was assaulted by a prisoner 'que puis son condemnation ject un brickbat a le dit justice que narrowly mist40.' It is as instructive as it is surprising that this jargon should have been written in a country where Frenchmen had long been regarded as hereditary foes. This prepares us for the remark that taught law is tough law. But when 'Dunce' had been set in Bocardo (and it was a doctor of the civil law who set him there41), why should the old law books be spared? They also were barbarous; they also were sufficiently papistical.

Turning to a more serious aspect of affairs, it would not I think be difficult to show that the pathway for a Reception was prepared. Not difficult but perhaps wearisome. At this point it is impossible for us to forget that the year 1485, if important to students of English history for other reasons, is lamentably important for this reason, that there Dr Stubbs laid down his pen. In his power of marshalling legal details so as to bring to view some living principle or some phase of national development he has had no rival and no second among Englishmen. Howbeit, we may think of the subjected church and the humbled baronage, of the parliament which exists to register the royal edicts, of the English Lex Regia which gives the force of statute to the king's proclamations42, of the undeniable faults of the common law, of its dilatory methods, of bribed and perjured juries, of the new courts which grow out of the King's Council and adopt a summary procedure devised by legists and decretists. Might not the Council and the Star Chamber and the Court of Requests—courts not tied and bound by ancient formalism,—do the romanizing work that was done in Germany by the Imperial Chamber Court, the Reichskammergericht43? This was the time when King Henry's nephew James V was establishing a new court in Scotland, a College of Justice, and Scotland was to be the scene of a Reception44.

It seems fairly certain that, besides all that he effected, Henry had at times large projects in his mind: a project for a great college of law (possibly a College of Justice in the Scotch sense), a project for the reformation of the Inns of Court, which happily were not rich enough to deserve dissolution45, also perhaps a project for a civil code as well as the better known project for a code ecclesiastical. In Edward VI's day our Regius and German Professor of Divinity, Dr Martin Butzer, had heard, so it seems, that such a scheme had been taken in hand, and he moved in circles that were well informed. He urged the young Josiah to go forward in the good work; he denounced the barbarism of English law and (to use Bentham's word) its incognoscibility46. The new ecclesiastical code, as is generally known, was never enacted; but we know equally well that the draft is in print. Its admired Latinity is ascribed to Prof. Smith's immediate successor, Dr Walter Haddon. I take it that now-a-days few English clergymen wish that they were living—or should I not say dying?—under Dr Haddon's pretty phrases47. Codification was in the air. Both in France and in Germany the cry for a new Justinian was being raised, and perhaps we may say that only because a new Justinian was not forthcoming, men endeavoured to make the best that they could of the old48. How bad that best would be Francis Hotman foretold.

And then we see that in 1535, the year in which More was done to death, the Year Books come to an end: in other words, the great stream of law reports that has been flowing for near two centuries and a half, ever since the days of Edward I, becomes discontinuous and then runs dry. The exact significance of this ominous event has never yet been duly explored; but ominous it surely is49. Some words that once fell from Edmund Burke occur to us: 'To put an end to reports is to put an end to the law of England50.' Then in 1547 just after King Henry's death a wail went up from 'divers students of the common laws.' The common laws, they said, were being set aside in favour of 'the law civil' insomuch that the old courts had hardly any business51. Ten years later, at the end of Mary's reign, we read that the judges had nothing to do but 'to look about them,' and that for the few practitioners in Westminster Hall there was 'elbow room enough52.' In criminal causes that were of any political importance an examination by two or three doctors of the civil law threatened to become a normal part of our procedure53. In short, I am persuaded that in the middle years of the sixteenth century and of the Tudor age the life of our ancient law was by no means lusty.

And now we may ask what opposing force, what conservative principle was there in England? National character, the genius of a people, is a wonder-working spirit which stands at the beck and call of every historian. But before we invoke it on the present occasion we might prudently ask our books whether in the sixteenth century the bulk of our German cousins inherited an innate bias towards what they would have called a Welsh jurisprudence. There seems to be plentiful evidence that the learned doctores iuris who counselled the German princes and obtained seats in the courts were cordially detested by the multitude. In modern times they often have to bear much blame for that terrible revolt which we know as the Peasants' War54. No doubt there were many differences between England and Germany, between England and France, between England and Scotland55. Let us notice one difference which, if I am not mistaken, marked off England from the rest of the world. Medieval England had schools of national law.

The importance of certain law schools will be readily conceded, even to one who is in some sort officially bound to believe that law schools may be important. A history of civilization would be miserably imperfect if it took no account of the first new birth of Roman law in the Bologna of Irnerius. Indeed there are who think that no later movement,—not the Renaissance, not the Reformation—draws a stronger line across the annals of mankind than that which is drawn about the year 1100 when a human science won a place beside theology. I suppose that the importance of the school of Bourges would also be conceded. It may be worth our while to remark that the school of Bologna had a precursor in the school of Pavia, and that the law which was the main subject of study in the Pavia of the eleventh century was not Roman law but Lombard law: a body of barbaric statutes that stood on one level with the Anglo-Saxon laws of the same age. This I say, not in order that I may remind you what sort of law it was that Archbishop Lanfranc studied when as a young man he was a shining light in the school of Pavia, but because this body of Lombard law, having once become the subject of systematic study, showed a remarkable vitality in its struggle with Roman jurisprudence. Those Italian doctors of the middle age who claimed for their science the fealty of all mankind might have been forced to admit that all was not well at home. They might call this Lombard law ius asininum and the law of brute beasts, but it lingered on, and indeed I read that it was not utterly driven from the kingdom of Naples until Joseph Bonaparte published the French code. Law schools make tough law56.

Very rarely do we see elsewhere the academic teaching of any law that is not Roman: imperially or papally Roman. As a matter of course the universities had the two legal faculties, unless, as at Paris, the Pope excluded the legists from an ecclesiastical preserve. The voice of John Wyclif pleading that English law was the law that should be taught in English universities was a voice that for centuries cried in the wilderness. It was 1679 before French law obtained admission into the French universities57. It was 1709 before Georg Beyer, a pandectist at Wittenberg, set a precedent for lectures on German law in a German university58 It was 1758 before Blackstone began his ever famous course at Oxford. The chair that I cannot fill was not established until the transatlantic Cambridge was setting an example to her elderly mother59. But then, throughout the later middle age English law had been academically taught.

No English institutions are more distinctively English than the Inns of Court; of none is the origin more obscure. We are only now coming into possession of the documents whence their history must be gathered, and apparently we shall never know much of their first days60. Unchartered, unprivileged, unendowed, without remembered founders, these groups of lawyers formed themselves and in course of time evolved a scheme of legal education: an academic scheme of the medieval sort, oral and disputatious. For good and ill that was a big achievement: a big achievement in the history of some undiscovered continents. We may well doubt whether aught else could have saved English law in the age of the Renaissance. What is distinctive of medieval England is not parliament, for we may everywhere see assemblies of Estates, nor trial by jury, for this was but slowly suppressed in France. But the Inns of Court and the Year Books that were read therein, we shall hardly find their like elsewhere. At all events let us notice that where Littleton and Fortescue lectured, there Robert Rede lectures, Thomas More lectures, Edward Coke lectures, Francis Bacon lectures, and highly technical were the lectures that Francis Bacon gave. Now it would, so I think, be difficult to conceive any scheme better suited to harden and toughen a traditional body of law than one which, while books were still uncommon, compelled every lawyer to take part in legal education and every distinguished lawyer to read public lectures. That was what I meant when I made bold to say that Robert Rede was not only an English judge but 'what is more' a reader in English law.

Deus bone! exclaimed Professor Smith in his inaugural lecture, and what excited the learned doctor to this outcry was the skill in disputation shown by the students of English law in their schools at London. He was endeavouring to persuade his hearers that in many ways the study of law would improve their minds. If, he urged, these young men, cut off as they are from all the humanities, can reason thus over their 'barbaric and semi-gallic laws,' what might not you, you cultivated scholars do if you studied the Digest and Alciatus and Zasius? And then the professor expressed a hope that he might be able to spend his vacation in the Inns of Court61. His heart was in the right place: in a school of living law. Even for the purposes of purely scientific observation the live dog may be better than the dead lion.

When the middle of the century is past the signs that English law has a new lease of life become many. The medieval books poured from the press, new books were written, the decisions of the courts were more diligently reported, the lawyers were boasting of the independence and extreme antiquity of their system62. We were having a little Renaissance of our own: or a gothic revival if you please. The Court of Requests in which Prof. Smith and Prof. Haddon had done justice was being tried for its life. Its official defender was, we observe, Italian by blood and Parisian by degree: Dr Adelmare, known to Englishmen as Sir Julius Caesar63. That wonderful Edward Coke was loose. The medieval tradition was more than safe in his hands. You may think it pleasant to turn from this masterful, masterless man to his great rival. It is not very safe to say what Thomas More did not know, less safe to say what was unknown to Francis Bacon, but I cannot discover that either of these scholars, these philosophers, these statesmen, these law reformers, these schemers of ideal republics, these chancellors of the realm, these law lecturers, had more than a bowing acquaintance with Roman law.

If Reginald Pole's dream had come true, if there had been a Reception— well, I have not the power to guess and you have not the time to hear what would have happened; but I think that we should have had to rewrite a great deal of history. For example, in the seventeenth century there might have been a struggle between king and parliament, but it would hardly have been that struggle for the medieval, the Lancastrian, constitution in which Coke and Selden and Prynne and other ardent searchers of mouldering records won their right to be known to school-boys. In 1610 when the conflict was growing warm a book was burnt by the common hangman: it was written by an able man in whom Cambridge should take some pride, Dr Cowell, our Regius Professor, and seemed to confirm the suspicion that Roman law and absolute monarchy went hand in hand64.

The profit and loss account would be a long affair. I must make no attempt to state it. If there was the danger of barbarism and stupidity on the one side, there was the danger of pedantry on the other: the pedantry that endeavours to appropriate the law of another race and galvanizes a dead Corpus Juris into a semblance of life. Since the first of January 1900 the attempt to administer law out of Justinian's books has been abandoned in Germany. The so-called 'Roman-Dutch' law of certain outlying parts of the British Empire now stands alone65, and few, I imagine, would foretell for it a brilliant future, unless it passes into the hand of the codifier and frankly ceases to be nominally Roman. Let us observe, however, that much had been at stake in the little England of the sixteenth century.

In 1606 Coke was settling the first charter of Virginia66. In 1619 elected 'burgesses' from the various 'hundreds' of Virginia were assembling, and the first-born child of the mother of parliaments saw the light67. Maryland was granted to Lord Baltimore with view of frankpledge and all that to view of frankpledge doth belong, to have and to hold in free and common socage as of the castle of Windsor in the county of Berks, yielding yearly therefor two Indian arrows of those parts on the Tuesday in Easter week68. The port and island of Bombay in one hemisphere69, and in another Prince Rupert's land stretching no one knew how far into the frozen north were detached members of the manor of East Greenwich in the county of Kent70. Nearly twenty-five hundred copies of Blackstone's Commentaries were absorbed by the colonies on the Atlantic seaboard before they declared their independence. James Kent, aged fifteen, found a copy, and (to use his own words) was inspired with awe71; John Marshall found a copy in his father's library72; and the common law went straight to the Pacific73.

A hundred legislatures—little more or less—are now building on that foundation: on the rock that was not submerged. We will not say this boastfully. Far from it. Standing at the beginning of a century and in the first year of Edward VII, thinking of the wide lands which call him king, thinking of our complex and loosely-knit British Commonwealth, we cannot look into the future without serious misgivings. If unity of law—such unity as there has been—disappears, much else that we treasure will disappear also, and (to speak frankly) unity of law is precarious. The power of the parliament of the United Kingdom to legislate for the colonies is fast receding into the ghostly company of legal fictions. Men of our race have been litigious; the great Ihering admired our litigiousness74; it is one of our more amiable traits; but it seems to me idle to believe that distant parts of the earth will supply a tribunal at Westminster with enough work to secure uniformity. The so-called common law of one colony will swerve from that of another, and both from that of England. Some colonies will have codes75. If English lawyers do not read Australian reports (and they cannot read everything), Australian lawyers will not much longer read English reports.

Still the case is not yet desperate. Heroic things can be done by a nation which means to do them: as witness the mighty effort of science and forbearance which in our own time has unified the law of Germany, and, having handed over the Corpus Juris to the historians, has in some sort undone the work of the Reception76. Some venerable bodies may understand the needs of the time, or, if I may borrow a famous phrase, 'the vocation of our age for jurisprudence and legislation.' Our parliament may endeavour to put out work which will be a model for the British world. It can still set an example where it can no longer dictate, and at least it might clear away the rubbish that collects round every body of law. To make law that is worthy of acceptance by free communities that are not bound to accept it, this would be no mean ambition. Nihil aptius, nihil efficacius ad plures provincias sub uno imperio retinendas et fovendas77. But it is hardly to parliament that our hopes must turn in the first instance. Certain ancient and honourable societies, proud of a past that is unique in the history of the world, may become fully conscious of the heavy weight of responsibility that was assumed when English law schools saved, but isolated, English law in the days of the Reception. In that case, the glory of Bourges, the glory of Bologna, the glory of Harvard may yet be theirs78.

NOTES

Sir R. Rede's Lectures.

1. Robert Rede was Autumn Reader at Lincoln's Inn in 1481, Lent Reader in 1485: Black Book of Lincoln's Inn, vol. I., pp. 71, 83.

2. Creighton, The Early Renaissance in England, Camb. 1895.

3. Coke, Introductory Letter to Part 10 of the Reports, and Preface to First Institute.

English law and the Renaissance.

4. Sohm, Fränkisches Recht und romisches Recht, 1880, p. 77: '...Thatsachen in Folge deren die Renaissance an dem englischen Rechtsleben so gut wie spurlos vorüberging.'

Sir T. More's Lectures.

5. Thomas More was Autumn Reader in 1511, Lent Reader in 1515: Black Book of Lincoln's Inn, vol. I., pp. 162, 175.

The Renaissance and Roman law.

6. Étienne Pasquier, Recherches sur la France, IX. 39 (cited by Dareste, Essai sur François Hotman, Paris, 1850, p. 17): 'Le siècle de l'an mil cinq cens nous apporta une nouvelle estude de loix qui fut de faire un manage de l'estude du droict avec les lettres humaines par un langage latin net et poly: et trouve trois premiers entrepreneurs de ce nouveau mesnage, Guillaume Budé, François, enfant de Paris, André Alciat, Italien Milanois, Udaric Zaze, Alleman né en la ville de Constance.' Savigny, Geschichte des römischen Rechts im Mittelalter, ed. 2, vol. {{sc}vi}}., p. 421: 'Nun sind es zwei Männer, welche als Stifter und Führer der neuen Schule angesehen werden können: Alciat in Italien und Frankreich, Zasius in Deutschland. Die ersten Schriftcn, worin die neue Methode erscheint, fallen in das zweite Decennium des fünfzehnten Jahrhunderts.'

Alciato and Zäsi. Andrea Alciato was born at Alzate near Milan in 1492, studied at Pavia and Bologna, in 1518 was called to teach at Avignon, went to Milan in 1520, to Bourges in 1528, was afterwards at Pavia, Bologna and Ferrara, died at Pavia in 1550 (Pertile, Storia del diritto italiano, ed. 2, vol. ii. (2), p. 428). Ulrich Zäsi was born in 1461, studied at Tübingen and at Freiburg where he became town-clerk and afterwards professor of law, died in 1535. See Stintzing, Ulrich Zasius, Basel, 1857, where (pp. 162—216) the intercourse between Erasmus, Zäsi, Alciato and Budé is described. The early Italian humanists had looked on jurisprudence with disdain and disgust. See Geiger, Renaissance und Humanismus, 1882, pp. 500—503; Voigt, Die Wiederbelebung des classischen Alterthums, ed. 3, vol. ii., pp. 477—484. Gradually, so I understand, philologians such as Budé (d. 1540) began to discover that there was matter interesting to them in the Corpus Juris, and a few jurists turned towards the new classical learning. See Tilley, Humanism under Francis I., in English Historical Review, vol. xv., pp. 456 ff. In 1520 Zäsi, writing to Alciato, said 'All sciences have put off their dirty clothes: only jurisprudence remains in her rags.' (Stintzing, Ulrich Zasius, p. 107.)

Rabelais and the commentators.

7. Rabelais, Pantagruel, liv. ii., ch. x.: 'Sottes Rabelais and et desraisonnables raisons et ineptes opinions de Accurse, Balde, Bartole, de Castro, de Imola, Hippolytus, Panorme, Bertachin, Alexander, Curtius et ces autres vieux mastins, qui jamais n'entendirent la moindre loy des Pandectes, et n'estoient que gros veaulx de disme, ignorans de tout ce qu'est necessaire à l'intelligence des loix. Car (comme il est tout certain) ilz n'avoient cognoissance de langue ny grecque, ny latine, mais seulement de gothique et barbare…Davantage, veu que les loix sont extirpées du milieu de philosophie morale et naturelle, comment l'entendront ces folz, qui ont par Dieu moins estudié en philosophie que ma mulle. Au regard des lettres d'humanité et cognoissance des antiquités et histoires ilz en estoient chargés comme un crapaud de plumes, et en usent comme un crucifix d'un pifre, dont toutesfois les droits sont tous pleins, et sans ce ne peuvent estre entenduz.' W. F. Smith, Rabelais, vol. i., p. 257, translates the last sentence thus: ' With regard to the cultivated literature and knowledge of antiquities and history, they were as much provided with those faculties as is a toad with feathers and have as much use for them as a drunken heretic has for a crucifix.…'

Back to the texts!

8. Stintzing, Geschichte der deutschen Rechtswissenschaft, vol. i., p. 96: 'Man wird sich bewusst, dass nicht in der überlieferten Schulweisheit das Wesen der Wissenschaft stecke; dass es auch hier gelte, dem Rufe des Humanismus "zurück zu den Quellen!" zu folgen.'

The French school.

9. The greatest names appear to be those of François Duaren or more

correctly Le Douarin (1509—1559), Jacques Cujas (1522—1590), Hugues Doneau (Donellus, 1527—1592), François Baudouin (Balduinus, 1520—1573), François Hotman (1524—1591), Denis Godefroy (1549—1622), Jacques Godefroy(1587—1652). Besides these there is Charles Du Moulin (Molinaeus, 1500—1566) whose chief work, however, was done upon French customary law, and who in the study of Roman law represents a conservative tradition. (Esmein, Histoire du droit français, ed. 2, p. 776.) Dareste (Essai sur François Hotman, p. 2) marks the five years 1546—1551 as those in which 'nos quatre grands docteurs du seizième siècle' (Hotman, Baudouin, Cujas, Doneau) entered on their careers.

New life of the Corpus Juris.

10. Viollet, Droit civil français, p. 25: 'C'est le mouvement scientifique de la Renaissance qui, semblable à un courant d'électricité, donne ainsi au vieux droit remain une vie nouvelle. Son autorité s'accroît par l'action d'une science, pleine de jeunesse et d'ardeur, d'une science qui, comme toutes les autres branches de l'activité humaine, s'épanouit et renaît.' Flach, in Nouvelle revue historique de droit, vol. vii., p. 222: 'En France Cujas porte à son apogée le renom de l'école nouvelle. Quelle autre préoccupation cette école pouvait-elle avoir que de faire revivre le véritable droit de la Rome ancienne, celui que la pratique avail touché de son souffle impur, celui qu'elle avait corrompu?'

Reginald Pole and the Reception.

11. Starkey's England, Early English Text Society, 1878, pp. 192 ff.; and see Letters and Papers, Henry VIII., vol. viii, pp. 81—84, and Ibid. vol. viii., pt. i, pp. xxxii—xxxiv. Thomas Starkey was employed in the endeavour to win Reginald Pole to King Henry's side in the matter of the divorce from Catherine and the consequent breach with Rome. The negotiation failed, but Starkey took the opportunity of laying before Henry a dialogue which he (Starkey) had composed. The interlocutors in this dialogue were Pole and the well-known scholar Thomas Lupset, and Pole was represented as expounding his opinions touching political and ecclesiastical affairs. How far at all points Starkey fairly represented Pole's views may be doubted. Still we have respectable evidence that Pole had talked in the strain of the following passage, and at any rate Starkey thought that in King Henry's eyes he was befriending Pole by making him speak thus.

Defects of English Law 'Thys ys no dowte but that our law and ordur thereof ys over-confuse. Hyt ys infynyte, and without ordur or end. Ther ys no stabyl grounde therin, nor sure stay; but euery one that can coloure reson makyth a stope to the best law that ys before tyme deuysyd. The suttylty of one sergeant schal enerte and destroy al the jugementys of many wyse men before tyme receyuyd. There is no stabyl ground in our commyn law to leyne vnto. The jugementys of yerys be infynyte and ful of much controuersy; and, besyde that, of smal authoryte. The jugys are not bounden, as I vnderstond, to folow them as a rule, but aftur theyr owne lyberty they haue authoryte to juge, accordyng as they are instructyd by the sergeantys, and as the cyrcumstance of the cause doth them moue. And thys makyth jugementys and processe of our law to be wythout end and infynyte; thys causyth sutys to be long in decysyon. Therefor, to remedy thys mater groundly, hyt were necessary, in our law, to vse the same remedy that Justynyan dyd in the law of the Romaynys, to bryng thys infynyte processe to certayn endys, to cut away thys long lawys, and, by the wysdome of some polytyke and wyse men, instytute a few and bettur lawys and ordynancys. The statutys of kyngys, also, be ouer-many, euen as the constytutyonys of the emperorys were. Wherefor I wold wysch that al thes lawys schold be brought into some smal nombur, and to be wryten also in our mother tong, or els put into the Latyn, to cause them that studye the cyuyle law of our reame fyrst to begyn of the Latyn tong, wherin they myght also afturward lerne many thyngys to helpe thys professyon. Thys ys one thyng necessary to the educatyon of the nobylyte, the wych only I wold schold be admyttyd to the study of thys law. Then they myght study also the lawys of the Romaynys, where they schold see al causys and controuersys decyded by rulys more conuenyent to the ordur of nature then they be in thys barbarouse tong and Old French, wych now seruyth to no purpos els. Thys, Mastur Lvpset, ys a grete blote in our pollycy, to see al our law and commyn dyscyplyne wryten in thys barbarouse langage, wych, aftur when the youth hath lernyd, seruyth them to no purpos at al; and, besyde that, to say the truth, many of the lawys themselfys be also barbarouse and tyrannycal, as you haue before hard. The wych al by thys one remedy Reception of the civil law recommended. schold be amendvd and correct, yf we myght induce the hedys of our cuntrey to admyt the same: that ys, to receyue the cyuyle law of the Romaynys, the wych ys now the commyn law almost of al Chrystyan natyonys. The wych thyng vndowtydly schold be occasyon of infynyte gudness in the ordur of our reame, the wych I coud schow you manyfestely, but the thyng hyt selfe ys so open and playn, that hyt nedyth no declaratyon at al; for who ys so blynd that seth not the grete schame to our natyon, the grete infamy and rote that remeynyth in vs, to be gouernyd by the lawys gyuen to vs of such a barbarouse natyon as the Normannys be? Who ys so fer from rayson that consyderyth not the tyranycal and barbarouse instytutionys, infynyte ways left here among vs, whych al schold be wypt away by the receyuyng of thys wych we cal the veray cyuyle law; wych ys vndowtydly the most auncyent and nobyl monument of the Romaynys prudence and pollycy, the wych be so wryte wyth such grauyte, that yf Nature schold herselfe prescrybe partycular meanys wherby mankynd schold obserue hyr lawys, I thynke sche wold admyt the same: specyally, yf they were, by a lytyl more wysedome, brought to a lytyl bettur ordur and frame, wych myght be sone downe and put in effect. And so ther aftur that, yf the nobylyte were brought vp in thys lawys vndoubtydly our cuntrey wold schortly be restoryd to as gud cyuylyte as there ys in any other natyon; ye, and peradventure much bettur also. For though thes lawys wych I haue so praysyd be commyn among them, yet, bycause the nobylyte ther commynly dothe not exercyse them in the studys thereof, they be al applyd to lucur and gayne, bycause the popular men wych are borne in pouerty only doth exercyse them for the most parte, wych ys a grete ruyne of al gud ordur and cyuylyte. Wherefor, Master Lvpset, yf we myght bryng thys ij. thyngys to effecte—that ys to say, to haue the cyuyle law of the Romaynys to be the commyn law here of Englond with vs; and, secondary, that the nobylyte in theyr youth schold study commynly therin—I thynk we schold not nede to seke partycular remedys for such mysordurys as we haue notyd before; for surely thys same publyke dyscyplyne schold redresse them lyghtly; ye, and many other mow, the wych we spake not yet of at al.'

Lupset thereupon objects that, seeing we have so many years been governed by our own law, it will be hard to bring this reform to pass. Pole replies that the goodness of a prince would bring it to pass quickly: 'the wych I pray God we may onys see.'

Pole and the reform of the land laws. The Pole of the Dialogue wished to make the power to entail lands a privilege of the nobility. A project of this kind had been in the air: perhaps in King Henry's mind. See Letters and Papers, Henry VIII., vol. iv., pt. 2, p. 2693 (A.D. 1529): 'Draft bill...proposing to enact that from 1 Jan. next all entails be annulled and all possessions be held in fee simple...The Act is not to affect the estates of noblemen within the degree of baron.' This is one of the proposals for restoring the king's feudal revenue which lead up to the Statute of Uses: an Act whose embryonic history has not yet been written, though Dr Stubbs has thrown out useful hints. (Seventeen Lectures, ed. 3, p. 321.)

Starkey's legal studies. When Pole left England in 1532 he went to Avignon where Alciato had lately been lecturing and became for a short while a pupil of Giovanni Francesco Ripa (Zimmermann, Kardinal Pole, 1893, p. 51), who was both canonist and legist. Whether at any time Pole made a serious study of the civil law I do not know. In 1534 Pole and Starkey were together at Padua; Pole was studying theology, Starkey the civil law. Starkey in a letter says 'Francis Curtius is dead, to the grief of those who follow the doctrine of Bartholus.' Perhaps we may infer from this that Starkey was in the camp of the Anti-Bartolists (Letters and Papers, Henry VIII., vol. VII., p. 331). In 1535 he says that he has been studying the civil law in order to form 'a better judgment of the politic order and customs used in our country' (Ibid. vol. VIII., p. 80).

The Reception in Germany.

12. For a general view of the Reception in Germany with many references

to other books, see Schroder, Deutsche Rechtsgeschichte, ed. 2, pp. 743 ff.; ed. 3, pp. 767 ff.

Modern estimates of the Reception.

13. For a moderate defence of the Reception, see Windscheid, Pandektenrecht, ed. 7, vol. I., pp. 23 ff. (§ 10). Ihering appeals from Nationality to Universality (cosmopolitanism); Geist des römischen Rechts, ed. 5, vol. I., p. 12: 'So lange die Wissenschaft sich nicht entschliesst, dem Gedanken der Nationalitat den der Universalität als gleichberechtigten zur Seite zu setzen, wird sie weder im Stande sein die Welt, in der sie selber lebt, zu begreifen, noch auch die geschehene Reception des romischen Rechts wissenschaftlich zu rechtfertigen.' The following sentences may, I believe, be taken as typical of much that has been written of late years. Brunner, Grundzüge der deutschen Rechtsgeschichte, 1901, p. 231: 'Allein was stets Tadel und Vorwurf hervorrufen wird, ist die Art, wie die Rezeption…durchgeführt wurde. Ein nationales Unglück war jenes engherzige Ignorieren des deutschen Rechts, jenes geistlose und rein äusserliche Aufpfropfen römischer Rechtssätze auf einheimische Verhältnisse, die Unkenntnis des Gegensatzes zwischen diesen und dem römischen Rechte, welche taub machte gegen die Wahrheit, dass kein Volk mit der Seele eines anderen zu denken vermag.'

Public reading of the canon law forbidden.

14. Injunctions of 1535, Stat. Acad. Cantab, p. 134: 'Quare volumus ut deinceps nulla legatur palam et publice lectio per academiam vestram totam in iure canonico sive pontificio nee aliquis cuiuscunque conditionis homo gradum aliquem in studio illius iuris pontificii suscipiat aut in eodem inposterum promoveatur quovis modo.' See Mullinger, Hist. Univ. Camb. vol. I., p. 630; Cooper, Annals of Cambridge, vol. I., p. 375; and for Oxford, Ellis, Original Letters, Ser. II., vol. II., p. 60. In September 1535 Legh and Ap Ryce declare that the canon laws are 'profligate out of this realm.' (Letters and Papers, Henry VIII., vol. IX., p. 138.)

Despite a doubt suggested by Stubbs (Seventeen Lectures, ed. 3, p. 368), I cannot believe that the slightest hint of a degree in canon law lurks at Cambridge in the title 'Legum Doctor' (LL.D.): not even 'a shadowy presentment of the double honour.' See E. C. Clark, Cambridge Legal Studies, 1888, pp. 56 ff., where that title is well explained. On the continent a settled usage contrasted the doctores legum and the doctores decretorum. See e.g. Stintzing, Geschichte der deutschen Rechtswissenschaft, vol. I., p. 25: 'In Italien hatten die Legisten und Decretisten verschiedene Schulen gebildet. In Deutschland waren sie zwar zu einer Facultät vereinigt, bildeten jedoch lange Zeit zwei getrennte Abtheilungen, von denen jede ihre eigenen akademischen Grade ertheilte. Neben einander erscheinen die Doctores Legum und Doctores Decretorum, bis seit dem Anfang des 16. Jahrhunderts diese Scheidung schwindet und die Doctores utriusque iuris

immer häufiger und endlich zur Regel werden.'
Sir T. Smith.
15. See Mr Pollard's life of Smith in Dict. Nat. Biog. Some important facts, especially about his ordination, were revealed by J. G. Nichols, in Archaeologia, XXXVIII. 98-127.
Smith and the new jurisprudence.
16. Smith says that when he first became a member of the senate at Cambridge he bought the Digest and Code and certain works of Alciatus, Zasius and Ferrarius. (See Mullinger, History of the University of Cambridge, vol. II., p. 130.) Ferrarius is, I suppose, Arnaud Ferrier, the master of Cujas. Mr Mullinger (p. 126) suggests that the Spaniard Ludovico Vives while resident at Oxford may have propagated dissatisfaction with the traditional teaching of Roman law.
The Court of Requests.
17. Select Cases in the Court of Requests (Selden Society), 1898, p. cxxiii. Mr Leadam's introduction to this volume contains a great deal of new and valuable matter concerning this important court. The title of the 'masters of requests' seems certainly to come hither from France. Just at this time there was a good deal of borrowing in these matters: witness the title of the ' secretaries of state,' which, it is said, spreads outwards from Spain to make the tour of the world.
Smith's inaugural orations.
18. Of Smith's two orations there is a copy in Smith's Camb. Univ. Libr. Baker MSS. XXXVII. 394, 414. Mr Mullinger (Hist. Univ. Cambr., vol. II., p. 127) has given an excellent summary. The following passage is that in which the Professor approaches the question whether in England there is a career open to the civilian. He has been saying that we ought not to study merely for the sake of riches. 'Tamen si qui sint qui hoc requirant, sunt archiva Londini, sunt pontificia fora, forum est praefecti quoque classis, in quibus proclamare licet et vocem vendere; est scriptura; singuli pontifices cancellarios suos habent et officiales et commissarios, qui propter civilis et pontificii iuris professionem in hunc locum accipiuntur.' The orator proceeds to ask whether there is any youth who ungratefully thinks that proficiency in legal science will not find an adequate reward. 'In quo regno aut in cuius regis imperio tarn stulta ilium opinio tenebit? In hoccine nobilissimi atque invictissimi nostri principis Henrici octavi regno, cuius magnificentia in bonas literas, studiumque in literatos, omnium omnis memoriae principum facta meritaque superavit, cuius ingentia in academias beneficia, licet nulla unquam tacebit posteritas, tamen omni celebratione maiora reperientur. Cum strenue laboraveris et periculum ingenii tui feceris, teque non lusisse operam sed dignum aliquo operae precio et honore ostenderis, cur dejicies animum? Cur desperatione conflictabis? Cur de tanto fautore ingeniorum, tarn insigni bonae indolis exploratore, tarn

potenti Rege, tam munifico, tarn liberali et egregio amatore suorum demisse viliterque sentias?'

Diplomacy and the civil law. There follows much more flattery of the king as a patron of learning of every kind. 'Iuris quidem civilis consulti facultas in hac republica cum ad multos usus pernecessaria est, tum a principe nostro nequaquam negligi aut levem haberi, vel hoc argumento esse potest, quod tam amplo planeque regio stipendio et meam hic apud vos mediocritatem et alium Oxonii disertum ac doctum virum ius hoc civile praelegere profiterique voluit.' And the study of the civil law is the high road to diplomatic service. 'Ius vero civile sic est commune ut cum ex Anglia discesseris, nobiles, ignobiles, docti, indocti, sacerdotes etiam ac monachi cum aliquod specimen eruditionis videri volunt exhibuisse, nihil fere aliud perstrepunt quam quod ex hoc iure civili et pontificio sit depromptum.' The king has wisely employed civilians in his many legations. There follow compliments paid to Stephen Gardiner, Thomas Thirlby, William Paget, Thomas Wriothesley, and Thomas Legh. On the whole, the professor can hold out to his pupils the prospect of diplomatic employment, of masterships in the chancery ('sunt archiva Londini'), of practice in the ecclesiastical courts and the court of admiralty, and besides this they are to remember that the king is a great patron of learning. I do not see any hint that knowledge of Roman law will help a man at the bar of the ordinary English courts.

The rewards for civilians. For more of the attempt to put new life into the study of Roman law at Cambridge, see Mullinger, op. cit., vol. II., pp. 132 ff. Though Somerset desired to see a great civil law college which should be a nursery for diplomatists, the Edwardian or Protestant Reformation of the church was in one way very unfavourable to the study of the civil law. Bishoprics and deaneries were thenceforth reserved for divines, and thus what had been the prizes of his profession were placed beyond the jurist's reach. Dr Nicholas Wotton (d. 1567), dean of Canterbury and York, may be regarded as one of the last specimens of an expiring race. Men who were not professionally learned, men like Sir Francis Bryan (d. 1550) and Sir Thomas Wyatt (d. 1542), had begun to compete with the doctors for diplomatic missions and appointments. Also the chancellorship of the realm had come within the ambition of the common lawyer, and (though Bishop Goodrich may be one instance to the contrary) the policy which would commit the great seal to the hands of a prelate was the policy which would resist or reverse ecclesiastical innovations. Even the mastership of the rolls, which had been held by doctors of Padua and Bologna, fell to the common lawyers. Thomas Hannibal, master of the rolls (1523—1527), must, one would think, have been an Italian, as were the king's Latin secretaries Andrea Ammonio and Pietro Vannes.

The heathenry of the Digest.

19. See Janssen, Geschichte des deutschen Volkes, vol. I., pp. 471-501, where the cry of 'heathenry!' is raised against the civil law. Janssen's attempt to praise the canon law as radically Germanic while blaming the 'absolutistic' tendencies of the civil law seems strange. Was not the canon law, with its pope, qui omnia iura habet in scrinio pectoris sui, absolutistic enough?

Wyclif on English and Roman law.

20. Wyclif, Tractatus de officio regis, Wyclif Society, 1887, pp. 56, 193, 237, 250: 'Leges regni Anglie excellunt leges imperiales cum sint pauce respectu earum, quia supra pauca principia relinquunt residuum epikerie sapientum... Non credo quod plus viget in Romana civilitate subtilitas racionis sive iusticia quam in civilitate Anglicana...Non pocius est homo clericus sive philosophus in quantum est doctor civilitatis Romane quam in quantum est iusticiarius iuris Anglicani...Unde videtur quod si rex Anglie non permitteret canonistas vel civilistas ad hoc sustentari de suis elemosinis vel patrimonio crucifixi ut studeant tales leges...non dubium quin clerus foret utilior sibi et ad ecclesiasticam promocionem humilior ex noticia civilitatis proprie quam ex noticia civilitatis duplicis aliene.' By 'the patrimony of the crucified' Wyclif means ecclesiastical revenues, which some of the bishops have been using in the endowment of legal studies at the universities: e.g. Bishop Bateman at Cambridge.

Wyclif and the law of the emperor. Wyclif, Select English Works, ed. Arnold, vol. III., p. 326: 'It were more profit boþe to body and soule þat oure curatis lerneden and tau☐ ten many of þe kyngis statutis, þan lawe of

þe emperour. For oure peple is bounden to Þe kyngis statutis and not to þe emperours lawe, but in as moche as it is enclosid in Goddis hestis. Þanne moche tresour and moch tyme of many hundrid clerkis in unyversite and

oÞere placis is foule wastid aboute bookis of þe emperours lawe and studie about hem....It semeþ þat curatis schulden raþere lerne and teche þe kyngis statutis, and namely þe Grete Chartre, þan þe emperours lawe or myche part of the popis. For men in oure rewme ben bounden to obeche to þe kyng and his ri☐ tful lawes and not so to þe emperours; and þei my☐ tten wonder wel be savyd, þou☐ many lawes of þe pope had nevere be spoken, in þis world ne þe toþere.'

Wyclif and paynim's law Wyclif, Unprinted English Works, Early English Text Society, 1880, p. 157: 'Þe fyue and twentiþe errour: þei chesen newe lawis maad of synful men and worldly and couetyse prestis and clerkis...for now heþenne mennus lawis and worldly clerkis statutis ben red in vnyuersitees, and curatis lernen hem faste wiþ grete desire, studie and cost...Ibid. p. 184:...lawieris maken process bi sotilte and cauyllacions of lawe cyule, þat is moche heþene mennus lawe, and not accepten the forme of þe gospel, as ☐ if þe gospel were no so good as paynymes lawe.' It is interesting to see Janssen's denunciation of Roman law as Pagan thus forestalled by the great heretic, in whose eyes the Decretals were but little, if at all, better than the Digest.

A. Agustin in England

21. For Antonio Agustin (born 1517, bishop of Alife 1556, bishop of Lerida 1561, archbishop of Tarragona 1576, died 1586) see Schulte, Geschichte der Quellen und Literatur des canonischen Rechts, vol. III., p. 723; Maasen, Geschichte der Quellen des canonischen Rechts, vol. I., pp. xix ff. His stay in England is attested in the Venetian Calendars, 1555—6, pp. 20, 24, 32, 34, 56, 166. See also Ibid., 1556—7, p. 1335. See also the funeral oration by And. Schott suffixed to Ant. Augustini De emendatione Gratiani dialogorum libri duo, Par. 1607, p. 320: 'Iulius tertius P. M....adeo Antonium dilexit ut et intimis consiliis adhibuerit, legatumque summa cum auctoritate in Britanniam insulam opibus florentissimam miserit, cum Rex vere Catholicus Philippus secundus Mariam reginam, Catholicorum regum Ferdinandi et Isabellae neptem, duxit uxorem. ...Anno 1555 revertit ex Anglia Romam Augustinus.' Apparently he was sent, not merely in order that he might congratulate Philip and Mary, but also that 'tanquam iurisconsultus legato adesset' (Schulte, op. cit., p. 724). He is charged by modern historians with not having spoken plainly all that he knew about the origin of the Pseudo-Isidorian decretals. England may have contributed a little towards the explosion of the great forgery by means of books that were lent to the Magdeburg Centuriators by Queen Elizabeth and Abp. Parker. See Foreign Calendar, 15612, pp. 117 9.

B. John Story.

22. See Mr Pollard's life of Story in Dict. Nat. Biog. See also Dyer's Reports, f. 300. On his arraignment for high treason Story ineffectually pleaded that he had become a subject of the king of Spain.

23. See Stintzing, Ulrich Zasius, pp. 216 ff.

Zasius and Luther.

24. Ranke, History of the Reformation in Germany (transl. Austin), vol. II., pp. 978.

The French lawyers and the Reformation

25 . The Nihil hoc ad edictum praetoris! is currently ascribed to Cujas, but the ultimate authority for the story I do not know. See Brissaud, Histoire du droit français, p. 355: 'La science laïque déclarait par la bouche d'un de ses plus grands représentants qu'elle n'e'tait plus l'humble servante de la théologie; elle affirmait sa sécularisation.' It seems that Cujas ('wie beinahe alle Rechtsgelehrten seiner Zeit') at first sided with the Reformers, but that he afterwards, at least outwardly, made his peace with the Catholic church (Spangenberg, Jacob Cujas und seine Zeitgenossen, Leipz. 1822, p. 162; Haag, La France protestante, ed. 2, vol. iv., col. 957 970). Doneau was a Calvinist; driven from France by Catholics and from Heidelberg by

Lutherans, he went to Leyden and ultimately to Altdorf. Hotman was a Calvinist, intimately connected with the church of Geneva. Baudouin was compelled to leave France for Geneva, whence he went to Strassburg and Heidelberg; but he quarrelled with Calvin and was accused of changing his religion six times. Charles Du Moulin also had been an exile at Tubingen. It is said that after a Calvinistic stage he became a Lutheran; on his death-bed he returned to Catholicism: such at least was the tale told by Catholics. (See Brodeau, La vie de Maistre Charles Du Molin, Paris, 1654; Haag, La France protestante, ed. 2, vol. V., col. 783 789.) To say the least, he had been 'ultra-gallican.' (Schulte, Geschichte der Quellen des canonischen Rechts, vol. iv., p. 251.) Of Le Douaiin also it is said 'il était réformé de coeur 5 (La France protestante, ed. 2, vol. v., col. 508). 'Die grosse Mehrzahl der hervorragenden Juristen bekannte sich mit grosserer oder geringerer Entschiedenheit zur Partei der Hugenotten' (Stintzing, Geschichte der deutschen Rechtsivissenschaft, vol. I., p. 372).

26. Stintzing, Geschichte der deutschen Rechtswissenschaft, vol. I., p. 284.

Francis Hotman and England

27. Elizabeth's invitation to Hotman is mentioned in the Elogium of him prefixed to his Opera (1599), p. viii, and in Dareste's essay (p. 5). His son John spent some time at Oxford. In 1583 John tells his father that at Oxford he has plenty of time for study 'quamvis hic miris modis frigeat iuris civilis studium et mea hac in re opera nemini grata possit esse in Anglia' (Hotomanorum Epistolae, Amstd., 1620, p. 325). In 1584 John was consulted along with Alberigo Gentili by the English government in the Mendoza case (Holland, Albericus Gentilis, pp. 14, 15). There is nothing improbable in the story that Francis was offered a post at Oxford. He must have been well known to Cecil. In 1562 he was active in bringing Conde into touch with Elizabeth and so in promoting the expedition to Havre. Conde's envoy brought to Cecil a letter of introduction from Hotman (Foreign Calendar, 1561 2, p. 601). Baudouin also at this time was making himself useful to the English government. (See e.g. Foreign Calendar, 1558 9, p. 173; 1561 2, pp. 60, 367, 454, 481, 510.) It has been said that Queen Elizabeth spoke of Charles Du Moulin as her kinsman (Brodeau, Vie de C. Du Molin, p. 4). Whether in the pedigree of the Boleyns there is any ground for this story I do not know. See La France protestante, ed. 2, vol. v., col. 783. Sir Thomas Craig, who is an important figure in the history of Scotch law, sat at the feet of Baudouin, and Edward Henryson, who in 1566 became a lord of session, had been a professor at Bourges (Dict. Nat. Biog.).

Francis Hotman and Roman law.

28. The Epistre adressée au tygre de la France, a violent invective against the Cardinal of Lorraine, still finds admirers among students of French prose. Apparently Hotman would have been the last man to preach a

Reception of Roman law in England. Being keenly alive to the faults of Justinian's books, he resisted the further romanization of French law, demanded a national code, admired the English limited monarchy, and by his Franco-Gallia made himself in some sort the ancestor of the 'Germanists.' Some of these 'elegant' French jurists were so much imbued with the historical spirit that in their hands the study of Roman law became the study of an ancient history. The following words cited and translated by Dareste from Baudouin (François Hotman, p. 19) have a wonderfully modern sound: 'Ceux qui ont étudié le droit auraient pu trouver dans l'histoire la solution de bien des difficultés, et ceux qui ont écrit l'histoire auraient mieux fait d'étudier le développement des lois et des institutions, que de s'attacher à passer en revue les armées, à décrire les camps, à raconter les batailles, à compter les morts.' 'Sine historia caecam esse iurisprudentiam, disait Baudouin:' (Brissaud, Histoire dn droit français, p. 349).

Coke and Hotman.

29. Coke, Introductory Letter to Part 10 of the Reports, and Preface to Coke upon Littleton (First Institute). The words of Hotman which moved Coke to wrath will be found in De verbis feudalibus commentarius (F. Hotmani Opera, ed. 1599, vol. II., p. 913) s.v. feodum. Hotman remarks that the English use the word fee (longissime tamen a Langobardici iuris ratione et institute) to signify 'praedia omnia quae perpetuo iure tenentur.' He then adds that Stephanus Pasquerius (the famous Étienne Pasquier) had given him Littleton's book: 'ita incondite, absurde et inconcinne scriptum, ut facile appareat verissimum esse quod Polydorus Virgilius in Anglica Historia de iure Anglicano testatus est, stultitiam in eo libro cum malitia et calumniandi studio certare.' To a foreign 'feudist' Littleton's book would seem absurd enough, because in England the feudum had become the general form in which all land-ownership appeared. Brunner (Deutsche Rechtsgeschichte, vol. II., p. 11) puts this well: 'Wo jedes Grundeigentum sich in Lehn verwandelt, wird das Lehn, wie die Entwicklung des englischen Rechtes zeigt, schliesslich zum Begrifif des Grundeigentums.'

Polydore Virgil. I have not found in Polydore Virgil's History anything about Littleton. There is a passage however in lib. IX. (ed. Basil. 1556, p. 154) in which he denounces the unjust laws imposed by William the Conqueror and (so he says) still observed in his own day: 'Non possum hoc loco non memorare rein tametsi omnibus notam, admiratione tamen longe dignissimam, atque dictu incredibilem: eiusmodi namque leges quae ab omnibus intelligi deberent, erant, ut etiam nunc sunt, Normanica lingua scriptae, quam neque Galli nee Angli recte callebant.' Among the badges of Norman iniquity is trial by jury, which Polydore cannot find in the laws of Alfred. This Italian historiographer may well be speaking what was felt by many Englishmen in Henry VIII's day when he holds up to scorn and detestation 'illud terribile duodecim virorum iudicium.' Fisher and More were tried by jury.

Alberigo Gentili

30. For Gentili see Holland, Inaugural Lecture, 1874, and Dict. Nat. Biog. For his attack on canon law see De nuptiis, lib. I., c. 19. For his quarrel with the 'elegant' Frenchmen, see De iuris interpretibus dialogi sex. The defenders of the new learning and the mos Gallicus, as it was called, threw at their adversaries the word ' barbarian'; the retort of the conservative upholders of the mos Italicus was 'mere grammarian.' By expelling such men as the Gentilis, Italy forfeited her pre-eminence in the world of legal study. Nevertheless it is said that both in France and Germany the practical Roman law of the courts was for a long time the law of the 'Bartolist' tradition. Esmein (Histoire du droit français, ed. 2, p. 776) says: 'Cujas exerça sur le développement des théories de droit remain suivies en France une action beaucoup moins puissante que Du Moulin, et la filiation du romaniste Du Moulin n'est pas niable: par la forme comme par le fond, c'est le dernier des grands Bartolistes.'

Marsilianisni and Henricianism

31. Thomas Starkey, when he was trying to win over Reginald Pole to Henry's side, wrote thus: 'Thes thyngs I thynke schal be somewhat in your mynd confermyd by the redyng of Marsilius, whome I take, though he were in style rude, yet to be of grete iugement, and wel to set out thys mater, both by the authoryte of scripture and good reysonys groundyd in phylosophy, and of thys I pray you send me your iugement.' (Starkey's England, Early Engl. Text Soc. 1878, p. xxv.) Chapuis (the imperial ambassador at Henry's court) to Charles V, 3 Jan. 1534 (Letters and Papers of Henry VIII., vol. VII., p. 6): ' The little pamphlet composed by the Council, which I lately sent to your Majesty, is only a preamble and prologue of others more important which are now being printed. One is called Defensorium Pacis, written in favour of the emperor Loys of Bavaria against apostolic authority. Formerly no one dared read it for fear of being burnt, but now it is translated into English so that all the people may see and understand it.' William Marshall to Thomas Cromwell (Ibid., p. 178): 'Whereas you promised to lend me £20 towards the printing of Defensor Pacis, which has been translated this twelve-month, but kept from the press for lack of money, in trust of your offer I have begun to print it. I have made an end of the Gift of Constantine and of Erasmus upon the Creed.' The 'Gift of Constantine' must be the famous treatise of Laurentius Valla. The translation of Marsilius appeared on 27 July, 1535 (Dict. Nat. Biog. s.n. William Marshall). In October twentyfour copies had been distributed among the Carthusians in London (Letters and Papers, vol. IX., p. 171). In 1536 Marshall complained that the book had not sold, though it was the best book in English against the usurped power of the bishop of Rome

(Ibid., vol. XL, p. 542). As to Byzantinism, if it be an accident it is a memorable accident that the strongest statement of King Henry's divinely instituted headship of the church occurs in a statute which enables unordained doctors of the civil (not canon) law to exercise that plenitude of ecclesiastical jurisdiction which God has committed to the king (Stat. 37 Hen. VIII., c. 17).

The Scotch Protestants and Justinian.

32. Foreign Calendar, 1558—9, p. 8. This seems to mean that the normal and rightful relation of church to state is that which is to be discovered in Justinian's books. If so, 'the Protestants of Scotland' soon afterwards changed their opinions under the teaching of Geneva and claimed for 'the estate ecclesiastical' a truly medieval independence.

The Henrician doctors of law.

33. The following facts are taken from the Dictionary of National Biography. Cuthbert Tunstall (afterwards bishop of Durham) 'graduated LL.D. at Padua.' Stephen Gardiner (afterwards bishop of Winchester) of Trinity Hall, Cambridge, 'proceeded doctor of the civil law in 1520 and of the canon law in the following year.... In 1524 he was appointed one of Sir Robert Rede's lecturers in the University.' Edmund Bonner of Broadgate Hall, Oxford, 'in 1519 he took on two successive days (12 and 13 June) the degrees of bachelor of civil and of canon law.... On 12 July, 1525, he was admitted doctor of civil law.' Thomas Thirlby (afterwards bishop of Ely) of Trinity Hall, Cambridge, 'graduated bachelor of the civil law in 1521 ... and proceeded doctor of the civil law in 1528 and doctor of the canon law in 1530.' Richard Sampson (afterwards bishop of Lichfield) of Trinity Hall, Cambridge, 'proceeded B.C.L. in 1505. Then he went for six years to Paris and Sens and returning proceeded D.C.L. in 1513.' John Clerk (afterwards bishop of Bath and Wells, Master of the Rolls), 'B.A. of Cambridge 1499 and M.A. 1502, studied law and received the doctor's degree at Bologna.' Richard Layton (afterwards dean of York) 'was educated at Cambridge, where he proceeded B.C.L. in 1522 and afterwards LL.D.' Thomas Legh of King's College(?), Cambridge, 'proceeded B.C.L. in 1527 and D.C.L. in 1531.' Instances of legal degrees obtained in foreign universities are not very uncommon. John Taylor, Master of the Rolls in 1527, 'graduated doctor of law at some foreign university, being incorporated at Cambridge in 1520 and at Oxford in 1522.' James Denton, dean of Lichfield, proceeded B.A. in 1489 and M.A. in 1492 at Cambridge. 'He subsequently studied canon law at Valencia in which faculty he became a doctor of the university there.' (For an earlier instance, that of Thomas Alcock of Bologna, see Grace Book A, Luard Memorial, p. 209. There are other instances in Boase, Register of the University of Oxford; consult index under Padua, Bologna, Paris, Orleans, Bourges, Louvain.)

'The king's great matter.' That wonderful divorce cause, which shook the world, created a large demand for the sort of knowledge that the university-bred jurist was supposed to possess, especially as a great effort was made to obtain from foreign doctors and universities opinions favourable to the king. The famous Cambridge 'Grecian' Richard Croke was employed in ransacking Italian libraries for the works of Greek theologians and in taking council with Hebrew rabbis. In Italy, France and Spain, as well as in England, almost every canonist of distinction, from the celebrated Philip Decius downwards, must have made a little money out of that law suit, for the emperor also wanted opinions.

Papists in the Inns of Court.

34. See the remarkable paper printed in Calendar of Inner Temple Records, vol. I., p. 470; also Mr Inderwick's preface pp. 1 ff. In 1570 Lincoln's Inn had not been exacting the oath of supremacy: Black Book, vol. I., pp. 369—372. See also the lives of Edmund Plowden, William Rastell and Anthony Browne (the judge) in Dict. Nat. Biog.: and for Browne see also Spanish Calendar, 1558—67, pp. 369, 640.

Sir T. Smith's 'Commonwealth'

35. Smith, Commonwealth of England, ed. 1601, p. 147: 'I haue declared summarily as it were in a chart or map, or as Aristotle termeth it ὡς ἐν τύπῳ the forme and maner of gouernment of England, and the policy therof, and set before your eyes the principall points wherin it doth differ from the policy or gouernment at this time vsed in France, Italy, Spaine, Germanie, and all other Countries, which doe follow the ciuill law of the Romaines, compiled by Iustinian into his pandects and code: not in that sort as Plato made his commonwealth, or Xenophon his kingdome of Persia, nor as Sir Thomas More his Vtopia, beeing fained commonwealths, such as neuer was nor neuer shall be, vaine imaginations, phantasies of Philosophers to occupie the time, and to exercise their wits: but so as England standeth, and is gouerned at this day the xxviij. of March. Anno 1565. in the vij. yeare of the raigne and administration thereof by the most vertuous and noble Queene Elizabeth, daughter to King Henry the eight, and in the one and fiftieth yeare of mine age, when I was Ambassadour for her Maiestie, in the Court of Fraunce, the Scepter whereof at that time the noble Prince and of great hope Charles Maximilian did holde, hauing then raigned foure yeares.'

Smith writes without books.

36. Smith to Haddon, 6 Ap. 1565, in G. Haddoni Smith writes Orationes, Lond. 1567, pp. 302-7: 'nostrarum legum ne unum quidem librum mecum attuli hic nee habebam iure consultos quos consulerem.' He has been telling how he wrote The Commonwealth of England.

Roman law on the Continent

37. From the time of Bracton to the present day Englishmen have often

allowed themselves phrases which exaggerate the practical prevalence of Roman law on the continent of Europe. Smith, for instance, who had been in many parts of northern France and as a learned and observant man, must have known that (to use Voltaire's phrase) he often changed law when he changed horses and that the Estates General had lately been demanding a unification of the divergent customs (Viollet, Histoire du droit civil français, p. 202; Planiol, Droit civil, 1900, vol. I., p. 16). Germans, who know what an attempt to administer Roman law really means, habitually speak of French law as distinctively un-Roman. Thus Rudolph Sohm (Fränkisches Recht und römisches Recht, Weimar, 1880, p. 76): 'die Gesetzbücher Napoleons I. zeigen, dass noch heute wenigstens das Privatrecht und Processrecht Frankreichs ein Abkömmling nicht des römischen, noch des italienischen, sondern des fränkischen Rechtes ist.' So Planiol (op. cit., vol. I., p. 26): 'Deux courants se sont trouvés en présence lors de l'unification du droit français: l'esprit romain et les traditions coutumières. Ce sont ces dernières qui l'ont emporté. Le Code a été rédigé à Paris, en plein pays coutumier; les conseillers d'État appartenaient en majorité aux provinces septentrionales; le parlement de Paris avait eu dans l'ancien droit un rôle prépondérant. Il n'y a donc rien d'étonnant à voir l'esprit des coutumes prédominer dans le Code; le contraire eût été un non-sens historique.' Until the other day it was, I believe, a common remark that the large part of Germany which stood under the French code either in a translated or untranslated form—and this part contained about one-sixth of the Empire's population—was the part of Germany in which the law was least Roman and most Germanic. The division of France into two great districts was not equal: before the acquisition of Elsass from Germany 'les pays de droit écrit comprenaient à peine les deux cinquièmes de la France' (Planiol, op. cit., vol. I., p. 11). See the useful map in Brissaud, Histoire du droit français, p. 152. Even in the south there was much customary law. A famous sentence in the custumal of Bordeaux placed 'the written law' below 'natural reason' (Viollet, op. cit., p. 150). Still it is not to be denied that a slow process of romanization—very different from the catastrophic Reception in Germany—went on steadily for some five or six centuries; and a system which as a whole seems very un-Roman to a student of what became 'the common law' of Germany may rightly seem Roman to an Englishman. Francis Bacon knew that France could not be compendiously described as a country governed by the civil law. In his speech on the Union of Laws (Spedding, Life and Letters vol. III, p. 337) he accurately distinguishes 'Gascoigne, Languedock, Provence, Dolphinie' which are 'governed by the letter or text of the civil law' from 'the Isle of France, Tourayne, Berry, Anjou and the rest, and most of all Brittain and Normandy,' which are 'governed by customs which amount unto a municipal law, and use the civil law but only for grounds and to decide new and rare cases.' English readers should at least know the doctrine, strongly advocated in modern Germany, that the private law which was developed in England by a French-speaking court was just one more French coutume. Sohm, Fränkisches Recht und römisches Recht, p. 69: 'Die Vorgeschichte des englischen Rechts von heute hat nicht in England, sondern in Nordfrankreich ihre Heimath....Stolz kann die Lex Salica auf die zahlreichen und mächtigen Rechte blicken, welche sie erzeugt hat.'

38. Blackstone, Commentaries, vol. III., p. 149; J. H, Tho. Mori Vita, Lond. 1652, p. 26.

39. Smith, Commonwealth, ed. 1601, p. 141: 'withernam...is in plaine Dutch and in our olde Saxon language wyther nempt.'

Barbarous language of the law.

40. Pollock, First Book of Jurisprudence, p. 283, from Dyer's Reports, 188b, in the notes added in ed. 1688: 'Richardson, ch. Just, de C. Bane, al Assises at Salisbury in Summer 1631. fuit assault per prisoner la condemne pur felony que puis son condemnation ject un Brickbat a le dit Justice que narrowly mist, and pur ceo immediately fuit indictment drawn per Noy envers le prisoner, and son dexter manus ampute and fix al Gibbet sur que luy mesme immediatment hange in presence de Court.' In France the Ordonnance of Villers-Cotterets (1539) decreed that the judgments of the French courts should be recorded no longer in Latin but in French. 'L'utilité de cette innovation...se comprend assez d'elle-même. On dit qu'un motif d'une autre nature, l'intérêt des belles-lettres, ne contribua pas moins à y decider le roi, choqué du latin barbare qu'employaient les tribunaux. Un arrêt rendu en ces termes: Dicta curia debotavit et debotat dictum Colinum de sua demanda, fut, dit on, ce qui entraîna la suppression du latin judiciaire.' Henri Martin, Histoire de France, vol. viii., pp. 272—3; see also Christie, Étienne Dolet, ed. 2, p. 424.

The fate of Duns Scotus.

41. Ellis, Original Letters, Ser. II., vol. ii., p. 61, of Dr Layton to Cromwell: 'We have sett Dunce in Bocardo and have utterly banished him Oxforde for ever, with all his blynd glosses, and is now made a common servant to evere man, fast nailede up upon posts in all common howses of easement.'

The English Lex Regia.

42. Stat. 31 Hen. VIII., cap. 8. Already in 1535 Cromwell reports with joy an opinion obtained from the judges to the effect that in a certain event the king might issue a proclamation which would be 'as effective as any statute' (Letters and Papers, Henry VIII., vol. viii., p. 411).

Civilians in councils and in courts.

43. The story (with which we are familiar in England) of the evolution of various councils and courts from an ancient Curia Regis seems to have a close parallel in French history: so close that imitation on one side or the other may at times be suspected. After the parlement with its various

chambers (which answer to our courts of common law) has been established, the royal council interferes with judicial matters in divers ways, and sections of the council become tribunals which compete with the parlement. (See, e.g. Esmein, Histoire du droit français, ed. 2, pp. 469 ff., and the pedigree of courts and councils in Lavisse et Rambaud, Histoire générale, vol. iv., p. 143; also the pedigree in N. Valois, Le conseil du roi (1888), p. 11; and Brissaud, Histoire du droit français, pp. 816 ff.) In Germany the doctors of civil law made their way first into councils and then into courts. 'Die fremdrechtlich geschulten Juristen wurden in Deutschland anfänglich nur in Verwaltungssachen verwendet. Zur Rechtsprechung gelangten sie dadurch, dass die Verwaltung diese an sich zog, und zwar zuerst am Hofe des Königs' (Brunner, Grundzüge der deutschen Rechtsgeschichte, 1901, p. 227). In the England of Henry VIII's day there seems no little danger that die fremdrechtlich geschulten Juristen, of whom there are a good many in the king's service, will gain the upper hand in the new courts that have emerged from the council, and will proceed from Verwaltung to Rechtsprechung. There came a time when Dr Tunstall (who got his law at Padua) was presiding over the Council of the North and Dr Roland Lee over the Council of the Marches. In 1538 Dr Lee, who was endeavouring to bring Wales to order, said in a letter to Cromwell, 'If we should do nothing but as the common law will, these things so far out of order will never be redressed; (Dict. Nat. Biog., vol. xxxii., p. 375).

Project for a new court. In 1534 there was a project for the erection of yet another new court. See Letters and Papers, Henry VIII., vol. VII., p. 603: 'Draft act of parliament for the more rigid enforcement of previous statutes, appointing a new court, to consist of six discreet men, of whom three at least shall be outer barristers in the Inns of Court, who shall be called justices or conservators of the common weal and sit together in the White Hall at Westminster or elsewhere, with power to discuss all matters relating to the common weal and to call before them all persons who have violated any act of parliament made since the beginning of Henry VIII.'s reign.' If only three of these judges need be barristers, what are the rest to be?

44 . Acts of the Parliament of Scotland, vol. II., p. 335.

Reform of the Inns of Court..

45. See the two papers that are printed by Waterhous, Fortescutus Restitutus, 1663, pp. 539, 543. In one of these Thomas Denton, Nicholas Bacon and Robert Cary are answering an inquiry addressed to them by Henry VIII touching the plan of legal education pursued in the Inns of Court. In this there are some phrases that tell of the revival of learning. The writers thank Almighty God for giving them a king 'endued and adorned himself with all kindes and sortes of good learning as well divine as

prophane' and one who 'purposeth to set forward and as it were to revive the study and perfect knowledge thereof, of long time detested and almost trodden under foot.' They remark also that many good and gentle wits have perished 'chiefly for that most of them in their tender years, indifferent to receive both good and bad, were so rooted and seasoned, as it were, in barbarous authors, very enemies to good learning, that hard it was, yea almost impossible, to reduce them to goodness.'

The king's College of Law. The other paper contains a project for the king's College of Law submitted by the same three writers. This looks like an attempt to obtain a royally endowed school of English law, and it is curious to observe that, not English, but good French is to take the place of bad French. ' The inner barristers shall plead in Latine, and the other barristers reason in French; and either of them shall do what they can to banish the corruption of both tongues.' One learned in French is 'to teach the true pronuntiation of the French tongue.' One of excellent knowledge in the Latin and Greek tongues is to read 'some orator or book of rhetoric, or else some other author which treateth of the government of a commonwealth, openly to all the company.' Students of this college are to be sent abroad to accompany ambassadors, and two students are to act as historiographers of the realm. Nothing is said of the civil law. On the whole, this seems to be a conservative proposal emanating from English barristers for bettering the education of the common lawyer, and thus rendering unnecessary such a Reception as Pole had proposed. We do not know that it represents Henry's thoughts. It was 'a civil law college' that Somerset wished to establish at Cambridge by a fusion of Trinity Hall and Clare. (See Mullinger, Hist. Univ. Camb., vol. II., pp. 134—137.)

Butzer on Henry VIII's project on codification.

46. Bucerus, De regno Christi, lib. II., cap. 56 (Scripta Anglica, Basil. 1577, p. 148): 'Passim enim queri bonos viros audio, leges regni huius decorum proprietatibus et commutationibus, de successionibus in bonis atque aliis huius generis civilibus contractibus et commerciis, esse perobscuras atque implicatas: adeoque etiam lingua perscriptas quadam obsoleta ut a nemine queant intelligi, qui non et eamn linguam didicerit et earum legum intelligentiam multo fuerit studio assecutus: indeque fieri ut plerique eorum qui eas leges aliquo modo habent cognitas, iurisque magis quam iusticiae sunt consulti, his ipsis legibus abutantur pro hominum decipulis retibusque pecuniarum. Quo regni non tolerando incommode permotum aiunt praestantissimum principem S. M. T. patrem ut corrigendis,elucidandisque his legibus certos pridem homines deputarit. Cum autem isti legum designati instauratores, vel mole operis absterriti, vel aliis impediti abstractique negociis, huic malo adhuc nullum attulerint remedium, abusioque et perversio legum indies magis invalescere dicatur, eo certe id erit S. M. T. et maturius et pertinacius elaborandum quo leges illae quam

rectissime ac planissime extent explicatae...Quid autem interest nullae existant leges, aut quae existunt sint civibus ignoratae?' Butzer, as this treatise shows, had some knowledge of the civil law, at least in the matter of divorce. He seems to think that a code for England might be so simple an affair that it could be put into rhyme and be sung by children. (See Mullinger, Hist. Univ. Camb., vol. II., p. 238.)
Codification of the ecclesiastical law.
47. Cardwell, The Reformation of the Ecclesiastical Laws, Oxf. 1850. See p. xxvi where Fox the martyrologist (1571) testifies to the beauty of Haddon's Latin, and then says: 'Atque equidem lubens optarim, si quid votis meis proficerem, ut consimili exemplo, nec dissimili etiam oratione ac stylo, prosiliat nunc aliquis, qui in vernaculis nostris legibus perpoliendis idem efficiat, quod in ecclesiasticis istis praestitit clarissimae memoriae hic Haddonus.' On the question as to the intended fate of heretics (including both Roman Catholics and Lutherans) under the Reformatio Legum, see Hallam, Const. Hist., ed. 1832, vol. I., p. 139; Maitland, Canon Law in England, p. 178.
The demand for Codification.
48. Commines attributes to Louis XI (circ. an. 1479) a project of reducing to uniformity all the customs of France. Francis Bacon more than once, when urging his schemes of law reform, referred to Louis's abortive project (Spedding, Life and Letters, vi. 66; VII. 362). Commines's story is not rejected by modern historians of French law. The official redaction of the various 'general customs' (customs of provinces) was commanded in 1453 by the ordinance of Montils-les-Tours. Little, however, was done in this matter until the reigns of Charles VIII and Louis XII. Many customs were redacted about the year 1510: that of Orleans in 1509; that of Paris in 1510. This might be described as a measure of codification: 'elle fit, des coutumes, de véritables lois écrites' or, as we might say, statute law. (Esmein, Histoire du droit français, 746 ff.; Viollet, Histoire du droit français) 142 ff.; Planiol, Droit civil, I. 12, 16). Then the Estates General at Orleans in 1560 in effect demanded a general code: 'Nous voulons une foy, une loy, un roy' said the prolocutor of the clergy. (Dareste, Hotman, p. 20.) Both Du Moulin and Hotman recommended codification and apparently thought that the task would not be difficult. (Viollet, op. cit., p. 209; Dareste, op. cit., p. 21.) Then as to Germany: 'An die Klagen über die Verwirrung, in welche das Recht durch die scholastische Wissenschaft gerathen ist, knüpft sich seit dem Anfange des 16. Jahrhunderts regelmässig das Verlangen, der Kaiser möge als ein neuer Justinian das gemeine Recht des Reichs zur Einfachheit und Klarheit gesetzlich reformiren...Das Verlangen nach einer Codification des gemeinen Rechts zieht sich durch das ganze 16. Jahrhundert.' (Stintzing, Geschichte der deutschen Rechtswissenschaft, vol. I., pp. 58 9.) In 1532 after a prolonged effort the Empire actually came by a criminal code, the

so-called Carolina (Constitutio Carolina Criminalis; die peinliche Halsgerichtsordnung Karls V.), but its operation was confined by a clause which sanctioned the ever increasing particularism of the various states by saving their ancient customs. (Ibid., pp. 621 ff.) Within some of these states or 'territories' there was in the sixteenth century a good deal of comprehensive legislation, amounting in some cases to the publication of what we might call codes. A Landrecht (to be contrasted with Reichsrecht) was issued by the prince. His legislative action was not always hampered by any assembly of Estates; he desired uniformity within his territory; and the jurists who fashioned his law-book were free to romanize as much as they pleased. The Würtemberg Landrecht of 1555 issued by Duke Christopher, a prince well known to Queen Elizabeth, is one of the chief instances (Stintzing, op. cit., vol. I., pp. 537 ff.; Schröder, Deutsche Rechtsgeschichte, ed. 3, pp. 886 ff.). The transmission of the cry for codification from Hotman to Leibnitz, and then to the enlightened monarchy of the eighteenth century is traced by Baron, Franz Hotmans Antitribonian, Bern, 1888. In Scotland also the Regent Morton (d. 1581) entertained a project of codification. A commission was appointed to prepare a uniform and compendious order of the laws. It seems to be a question among Scotch lawyers how far the book known as Balfour's Practicks represents the work of the commissioners. See Dict. Nat. Biog., vol. XV., p. 317; vol. III., p. 53.

The expiration of the Year Books.

49. The cessation of the Year Books in 1535 at the moment when the Henrician Terror is at its height is dramatically appropriate. A great deal, however, has yet to be done before the relevant facts will be fully known. Mr C. C. Soule's Year-Book Bibliography, printed in Harvard Law Review, vol. xiv., p. 557, is of high importance. If by 'the Year Books' we mean a series of books that have been printed, then the Year Books become intermittent some time before they cease. The first eleven years of Henry VIII are unrepresented, and there are gaps between years 14 and 18 and between 19 and 26. It remains to be seen whether there are MSS. more complete than the printed series. Then we have on our hands the question raised by what Plowden says in the Preface to his Commentaries touching the existence of official reporters. Plowden says that he began to study the law in 30 Hen. VIII, and that he had heard say that in ancient times there were four reporters paid by the king. His words make it clear that the official reporters, if they ever existed, came to an end some considerable time before 30 Hen. VIII. The question whether they ever existed cannot be raised here. Mr Pike's investigations have not, so I think, tended to bear out the tale that Plowden had heard; and if the king paid stipends to the reporters, some proof of this should be forthcoming among the financial records. The evidence of Francis Bacon is of later date and looks like a mere repetition of what Plowden said (Bacon, Amendment of the Law;

Spedding, Life and Letters, vol. v., p. 86).

Decline of law reports. But, be all this as it may, the fact seems clear that the ancient practice of law reporting passed through a grave crisis in the sixteenth century. We know the reign of Edward IV and even that of Edward II better than we know that of Edward VI. The zeal with which Tottell from 1553 onwards was printing old reports makes the dearth of modern reports the more apparent. Then Plowden expressly says that he reported 'for my private instruction only,' and Dyer's Reports (which comprise some cases too early to have been reported by him) were posthumously published. The total mass of matter from the first half of the century that we obtain under the names of Broke, Benloe, Dalison, Keilwey, Moore and Anderson is by no means large, and in many cases its quality will not bear comparison with that of the Year Books of Edward IV. (J. W. Wallace, The Reporters, ed. 4, Boston, 1882, is an invaluable guide; see also V. V. Veeder, The English Reports, in Harvard Law Review, vol. xv., p. i.)

Burke on law reports.

50. Burke, Report from Committee appointed to inspect the Lords' Journals: 'To give judgment privately is to put an end to reports; and to put an end to reports is to put an end to the law of England.'

The Students' petition in 1547.

51. Acts of the Privy Council, 1547—1550, pp. 48—50. Petition of divers students of the common laws to the Lord Protector and the Privy Council: 'Pleasith it your honorable Lordships to call to your remembrance that whereas the Imperial Crowne of this realme of Inglande and the hole estate of the same have been always from the beginning a Reame Imperial, having a lawe of itself called the Commen Lawes of the realme of Inglande, by which Lawe the Kinges of the same have as Imperial Governours thereof ruled and governed the people and subjectes in suche sorte as the like thereof hath nat been seen in any other.... So it is, if it like your good Lordships, that now of late this Commen Lawes of this realme, partely by Injunctions, aswel before verdictes, jugementes and execucions as after, and partly by writtes of Sub Pena issuing owte of the Kinges Courte of Chauncery, hath nat been only stayed of their directe course, but also many times altrid and violated by reason of Decrees made in the saide Courte of Chauncery, most grounded upon the lawe civile and apon matter depending in the conscience and discrecion of the hearers thereof, who being Civilians and nat lerned in the Comen Lawes, setting aside the saide Commen Lawes, determyne the waighty causes of this realme according either to the saide Lawe Civile or to their owne conscience; which Lawe Civile is to the subjectes of this realme unknowne, and they nat bounden ne inheritable to the same lawe, and which Jugementes and Decrees grownded apon conscience ar nat grounded ne made apon any Incroachment of the civil

law. rule certeine or lawe written....And for a more amplyfyeng and inlarging of the jurisdiction of the saide Courte of Chauncery and derogacion of the saide Comen Lawes there is of late a Commission made contrary to the saide Commen Lawes unto certaine persones, the more part whereof be Civilians nat learned in the saide Lawes of this realme, autorising them to heare and determyne all matters and cawses exhibited into the saide Courte of Chauncery, by occasion whereof the matters there do daily more and more increase, insomuch as very fewe matters be now depending at the Comen Lawes....And by reason thereof there hath of late growne such a discourage unto the studentes of the saide Commen Lawes, and the said Commen Lawes have been of late so little estemed and had in experience, that fewe have or do regarde to take paynes of the profownde and sincere knolege of the same Lawe, by reason whereof there ar now very few, and it is to be doubted that within fewe yeares there shall nat be sufficient of lerned men within this realme to serve the king in that facultie. It therfore may please your honorable Lordships to make suche speady reformacion in the premisses as unto your Lordships shall seem moste mete and convenient.'

Civilians as judges. This petition led to the disgrace and punishment of the chancellor, the Earl of Southampton (Wriothesley), for having issued a commission without warrant and without consulting his fellow-executors of King Henry's will. With Somerset's motives for thrusting Southampton aside we are not concerned. (See Pollard, England under the Protector Somerset, pp. 31—33.) That he had any desire to protect the common lawyers we must not assume; but the petition itself deserves attention. The commissioners to whom Southampton had delegated judicial powers were Robert Southwell (master of the rolls), John Tregonwell, John Oliver, and Anthony Bellasyse (masters of chancery). Tregonwell, Oliver and Bellasyse were all doctors of the civil law (Dict. Nat. Biog.)

Common law and the Pilgrimage of Grace. In 1536 during the Pilgrimage of Grace one of the demands of the catholic insurgents was 'that the common laws may have place as was used at the beginning of the reign and that no injunctions be granted unless the matter has been determined in chancery.' This comes at the end of a long reactionary programme, which desires the restoration of the monasteries, of the papal supremacy and so forth: also the repeal of the statute 'That no man shall not will his lands'. The heretical bishops are to be burnt; Cromwell is 'to have condign punishment.' Also 'a man is to be saved by his book,' i.e. there is to be no infringement of the benefit of clergy. The heresies to be suppressed are those of 'Luther, Wyclif, Husse, Malangton, Elicampadus, Bucerus, Confessa Germaniae (Augsburg Confession], Apolugia Malanctons, the works of Tyndall, of Barnys, of Marshall, Raskell, Seynt Germayne and such other heresies of Anibaptist.' As I understand the protest against injunctions, it means that the chancery may interfere with an action at common law, only if that action is opening a question already decided in the chancery. It will be seen that in 1536 the cause of 'the common laws' finds itself in very queer company: illiterate, monkish and papistical company, which apparently has made a man of 'Anibaptist.' (For this important manifesto, see Letters and Papers, Henry VIII., vol. XI., pp. 506—507.)

Elbow-room in the courts of law.

52. Stow, Annals, ed. 1615, p. 631: 'This yeere (1557) in Michaelmas terme men might have scene in Westminster hall at the Kinges bench barre not two men of law before the iustices; there was but one named Fostar, who looked about and had nothing to doe, the iudges looking about them. In the common place no moe sergeants but one, which was sergeant Bouloise, who looked about him, there was elbow roome enough, which made the lawyers complaine of their iniuries in that terme.' In 1536 John Rastell the lawyer and printer of law books complains to Cromwell that in both capacities he is in a bad way: he used to print from two to three hundred reams every year but now prints not a hundred reams in two years; he used to make forty marks a year by the law and now does not make forty shillings (Ellis, Original Letters, Ser. III., vol. II., p. 309). On such stories as these little stress is laid; but until the judicial records of the Tudor reigns are statistically examined, scraps of information may be useful.

Examination by civilians in criminal cases.

53. For an instance see the examination of a servant of the Abbot of Sawley by Drs Layton, Legh and Petre (Letters and Papers, Henry VIII., vol. XII., pt. i, p. 231).

The doctors of law and the Peasants' War.

54. As to the evil done to the peasants in Germany by the Reception of Roman law, see Egelhaaf, Deutsche Geschichte (Zeitalter der Reformation), vol. i., pp. 544 ff.; Lamprecht, Deutsche Geschichte, vol. v., pp. 99 ff. Dr Brunner (Grundzüge der deutschen Rechtsgeschichte, 1901, p. 216) has lately said that Roman jurisprudence 'auch wenn sie nicht geradezu bäuernfeindlich war, doch kein Verständnis besass für die Mannigfaltigkeit der bäuerlichen Besitzformen des deutschen Rechtes.' One of the revolutionary programmes proposed an exclusion of all doctors of civil or canon law from the courts and councils of the princes. See Egelhaaf, op. cit., pp. 499, 598. The following is a pretty little tale:—' So geschah es wirklich einmal zu Frauenfeld im Thurgau, wo die Schöffen einen Doctor aus Constanz, der sich für die Entscheidung eines Erbschaftsstreites auf Bartolus und Baldus berufen wollte, zur Thüre hinauswarfen mit den Worten: "Hört ihr, Doctor, wir Eidgenossen fragen nicht nach dem Bartele und Baldele. Wir haben sonderbare Landbräuche und Rechte. Naus mit euch, Doctor, naus mit euch!" Und habe, heisst es in dem Berichte weiter, der gute Doctor müssen abtreten, und sie Amtleute haben sich einer Uriel

verglichen, den Doctor wieder eingefordert und ein Urtel geben wider den Bartele und Baldele und wider den Doctor von Constanz.' (Janssen, Geschichte des deutschen Volkes, vol. I., p. 490.) It is a serious question what would have become of our English copyholders if in the sixteenth century Roman law had been received. The practical jurisprudence of this age seems to have been kinder to the French than to the German peasant; perhaps because it was less Roman in France than in Germany. See E. Levasseur in Lavisse et Rambaud, Histoire générale, vol. iv., p. 188: 'Des jurisconsultes commencèrent à considérer l'inféodation comme une aliénation et le colon censitaire comme le véritable propriétaire de la terre sur laquelle le seigneur n'aurait possédé qu'un droit éminent? The true Romanist, I take it, can know but one dominium, and is likely to give that one to the lord.

England and Germany.

55. As regards Germany, the theoretical continuance of the Roman empire is not to be forgotten, but its influence on the practical Reception of Roman law may be overrated. In the age of the Reception Roman law came to the aid, not of imperialism, but of particularism. Then it is true that English law was inoculated in the thirteenth century when Bracton copied from Azo of Bologna. The effect of this is well stated by Dr Brunner in the inaugural address delivered by him as rector of the University of Berlin (Der Antheil des deutschen Rechtes an der Entwicklung der Universitäten, Berlin, 1896, p. 15): 'In England und Frankreich, wo die Aufnahme römischer Rechtsgedanken früher erfolgte, hat diese nach Art einer prophylactischen Impfung gewirkt und das mit ihnen gesättigte nationale Recht widerstandsfähig gemacht gegen zerstörende Infectionen.' As to the Roman law in Bracton, I may be allowed to refer to Bracton and Azo, Selden Society, 1895: in the introduction to that volume I have ventured to controvert some sentences that were written by Sir H. Maine. Bracton became important for a second time in the sixteenth century when (1569) his book was printed, for it helped Coke to arrange his ideas, as any one may see who looks at the margin of Coke's books. The medieval chancery has often been accused of romanizing. Its procedure was suggested by a summary procedure that had been devised by decretists and legists: the general aim of that scheme was the utmost simplicity and rapidity. (Contrast this summary procedure as revealed by Select Cases in Chancery, ed. Baildon, and Select Cases in the Court of Requests, ed. Leadam, with the solemn procedure of the civil law exemplified by Select Cases in the Court of Admiralty, ed. Marsden: these three books are published by the Selden Society.) On the other hand, no proof has been given that in the middle age the chancery introduced any substantive law of Roman origin. At a later time when it began to steal work (suits for legacies and the like) from the ecclesiastical courts, it naturally borrowed the rules by which those matters

had theretofore been governed.

The Reception in Scotland. A full history of the Reception in Scotland seems to be a desideratum. But see Goudy, Fate of Roman Law (Inaugural Lecture), 1894; also J. M. Irvine, Roman Law in Green's Encyclopedia of the Law of Scotland. Whether at any time the Reception in Scotland ran the length that it ran in Germany may be doubted; but the influence exercised by English example since 1603 would deserve the historian's consideration. Even if this influence went no further than the establishment of the habit of finding 'authority' in decided cases, it would be of great importance. Where such a habit is established in practice and sanctioned by theory, any return to the pure text, such as that which was preached in Germany by 'the historical school,' would be impossible. Also it may be suggested that the Roman law which played upon the law of Scotland in the seventeenth and eighteenth centuries was not always very Roman, but was strongly dashed with 'Natural Law.' For instance, if in Scotland the firm of partners is a 'legal person,' this is not due to the influence of Roman law as it is now understood by famous expositors, or as it was understood in the middle ages. Also (to take another example) it seems impossible to get the Scotch 'trust' out of Roman law by any fair process. The suggestion that it is 'a contract made up of the two nominate contracts of deposit and mandate' seems a desperate effort to romanize what is not Roman.

The persistence of Lombard law.

56. Fertile, Storia del diritto italiauo, ed. 2, vol. II. (2), p. 69: 'Laonde può dirsi che l'abrogazione definitiva ed espressa della legislazione longobardica nel regno di Napoli non abbia avuto luogo se non al principio del nostro secolo, sotto Giuseppe Bonaparte, al momento in cui vennero publicati cola i codici francesi.' On p. 65 will be found some of the opprobrious phrases that the civilians applied to Lombard law: 'nec meretur ius Lombardorum lex appellari sed faex': 'non sine ratione dominus Andreas de Isernia vocat leges illas ius asininum.'

French law in the universities.

57. Esmein, Histoire du droit français, ed. 2, p. 757: 'C'est seulement en 1679 que l'enseignement du droit français reçut une place bien modeste dans les universités.' Viollet, Histoire du droit civil français, p. 217: 'Lorsqu'en 1679, Louis XIV. érigea à la faculté de Paris une chaire de droit français et une chaire de droit romain, le premier professeur de droit français, Fr. de Launay, commenta les Institutes de Loisel, qui prirent ainsi une situation quasi-officielle à côté des Institutes de Justinien.' Brissaud, Histoire du droit français, p. 237: 'Le latin avait été jusque-là la langue de l'école. Le premier professeur en droit français à Paris, de Launay, fit son cours en langue française.'

German law in the universities.

58. Siegel, Deutsche Rechtsgeschichte, ed. 3, p. 152: Den ersten und

zugleich entscheidenden Schritt in dieser Richtung that Georg Beyer, welcher... zunächst durch einen Zufall veranlasst wurde, an der Wittenberger Universität, wohin er als Pandektist berufen worden war, 1707 eine Vorlesung über das ius germanicum anzukündigen und zu halten.'
Professorships in America.

59. Thayer, The Teaching of English Law at Universities in Harvard Law Review, vol. ix., p. 171: 'Blackstone's example was immediately followed here...In 1779...a chair of law was founded in Virginia at William and Mary College...and in the same year Isaac Royall of Massachusetts, then a resident in London, made his will, giving property to Harvard College for establishing there that professorship of law which still bears his name.' The Royall professorship was actually founded in 1815 (Officers and Graduates of Harvard, 1900, p. 24). At Cambridge (England) the Downing professorship was founded in 1800.

The Inns of Court.

60. See Records of the Honorable Society of Lincoln's Inn, 1896 ff.; Calendar of the Records of the Inner Temple, 1896. The records of Gray's Inn are, so I understand, to be published. See also Philip A. Smith, History of Education for the English Bar, 1860; Joseph Walton, Early History of Legal Studies in England, 1900, read at a meeting of the American Bar Association in 1899. In foreign countries there were gilds or fraternities of lawyers. Thus in Paris the avocats and procureurs about the middle of the fourteenth century formed a fraternity of St Nicholas: 'dont le chef porte le bâton ou banniere (de là le nom de bâtonnier)': Brissaud, Histoire du droit français, p. 898. But, though a certain care for the education of apprentices was a natural function of the medieval craft-gild, I cannot find that elsewhere than in England fraternities of legal practitioners took upon themselves to educate students and to give what in effect were degrees, and degrees which admitted to practice in the courts. R. Delachenal, Histoire des avocats au parlement de Paris (Paris, 1885), says that, though not proved, it is probable that already in the fourteenth and fifteenth centuries the avocat had to be either licencié en lois or licencié en décret: in other words, a legal degree given by an university was necessary for the intending practitioner. As regards the England of the same age two interesting questions might be asked. Was there any considerable number of doctors or bachelors of law who were not clergymen? Had the English judge or the English barrister usually been at an university? I am inclined to think that a negative answer should be given to the first question and perhaps to the second also. Apparently Littleton (to take one example) is not claimed by Oxford or Cambridge.

Sir T. Smith and the Inns of Court.

61. Smith, Inaugural Oration, MS. Baker, XXXVII. 409 (Camb. Univ. Lib.): '...At vero nostrates, et Londinenses iurisconsulti, quibuscum

disputare, cum ruri sim et extra academiam, non illibenter soleo, qui barbaras tantum et semigallicas nostras leges inspexerint, homines ab omnibus suis humanioribus disciplinis et hac academiae nostrae instructione semotissimi, etiam cum quid e philosophia, theologiave depromptum in quaestione ponatur, Deus bone! quam apte, quamque explicate singula resumunt, quanta cum facilitate et copia, quantaque cum gratia et venustate, vel confirmant sua, vel refellunt aliena! Certe nee dialecticae vim multum in eis desideres, nee eloquentiae splendorem. Eorum oratio est Anglicana quidem, sed non sordida, non inquinata, non trivialis, gravis nonnunquam et copiosa, saepe urbana et faceta, non destituta similitudinum et exemplorum copia, lenis et aequabilis, et pleno velut alveo fluens, nusquam impedita. Quae res tantam mihi eorum hominum admirationem concitavit, ut aliquandiu vehementer optarim, secessionem aliquam ab ista academia facere et Londinum concedere, ut eos in suis ipsis scholis ac circulis disputantes audirem, quod an sim facturus aliquando, cum feriae longae, et quasi solenne iusticium, nostris praelectionibus indicatur, haud equidem pro certo affirmaverim.'

Multiplication of English law books.

62. Soule, Year Book Bibliography, in Harvard Law Review, vol. XIV., p. 564: 'In 1553 the field of Year-Book publication was entered by Richard Tottell, who for thirty-eight years occupied it so fully as to admit no rival. There are about 225 known editions of separate Years or groups of Years which bear his imprint or can be surely attributed to his press...He is pre-eminently the publisher of Year Books, and he so completely put them 'in print' and so cheapened their price that he evidently made them a popular and profitable literature.'

In 1550 an English lawyer's library of printed books might apparently have comprised (besides some Statutes and Year Books) Littleton's Tenures, The Old Tenures, Statham's Abridgement, Fitzherbert's Abridgement, Liber Intrationum, The Old Natura Brevium, perhaps a Registrum Brevium (if that book, printed in 1531, was published before 1553), Institutions or principal grounds etc., Carta feodi simplicis, New book of presidentes, Diversite de courts, Novae Narrationes, Articuli ad novas narrationes, Modus tenendi curiam baronis, Modus tenendi unum hundredum, Fitzherbert's Justice of the Peace, Perkins's Profitable Book, Britton, Doctor and Student. A great part of what was put into print was of medieval origin and had been current in manuscript. In 1600 the following might have been added: Glanvill, Bracton, Fitzherbert's Natura Brevium, Broke's Abridgement, Broke's New Cases, Rastell's Entries, Staundford's Prerogative and Pleas of the Crown, Crompton's Justice of the Peace, Crompton's Authority of Courts, West's Symbolæography, Theloall's Digest, Smith's Commonwealth, Lambard's Archaionomia and Eirenarcha, Fulbecke's Direction or Preparative to the Study of the Law, Plowden's

Commentaries, Dyer's Reports and the first volume of Coke's Reports. This represents a great advance. Already Fulbecke in his curious book (which was reprinted as still useful in 1829) attempts a review of English legal literature: a critical estimate of Dyer, Plowden, Staundford, Perkins and other writers. Lambard's revelation of the Anglo-Saxon laws was not unimportant, for a basis was thus laid for national boasts; and, but for the publication of Glanvill, Bracton and Britton, the work that was done by Coke would have been impossible.

Were any books about Roman law printed in England before 1600, except a few of Gentili's?

The Court of Requests.

63. See Mr Leadam's Introduction to Select Pleas in the Court of Requests (Seld. Soc.) and Dict. Nat. Biog. s.n. Caesar, Sir Julius.

Cowell's 'Interpreter.'

64. See Gardiner, Hist. England, 1603—1642, vol. II., pp. 66—68. E. C. Clark, Cambridge Legal Studies, pp. 74—75. Cowell's Institutions (less known than the Interpreter) are an attempt, 'in the main very able,' so Dr Clark says, to bring English materials under Roman rubrics. It is a book which might have played a part in a Reception; but it came too late.

Roman-Dutch law.

65. There can now be few, if any, countries outside law - the British Empire in which a rule of law is enforced because it is (or is deemed to be) a rule of Roman law. See Galliers v. Rycroft A. C. 130, for a recent discussion before the Judicial Committee (on an appeal from Natal) of the import of a passage in the Digest. Are there many lands in which so much respect would be paid by a tribunal and for practical purposes to a response of Papinian's? I think not.

First Charter of Virginia.

66. Macdonald, Select Charters, 1899, p. 1: 'The first draft of the charter...was probably drawn by Sir John Popham...but the final form was the work of Sir Edward Coke, attorney general, and Sir John Dodderidge, solicitor general.'

First Assembly in Virginia.

67. Doyle, The English in America, vol. I., p. 211: First Assembly 'On the 30th of July, 1619, the first Assembly met in the little church at Jamestown. A full report of its proceedings still exists in the English Record Office (Colonial Papers, July 30, 1619).' An abstract is printed in Calendar of State Papers, Colonial, 1574—1660, p. 22.

The tenure of Maryland.

68. Charter of Maryland, 1632, Macdonald, Select Charters, p. 53. In 1620 the grant to the Council of New England (Ibid., p. 23) referred to the manor of East Greenwich and reserved by way of rent a fifth part of the ore of gold and silver. The grant of Carolina (Ibid., p. 121) reserved a rent

of twenty marks and a fourth of the ore. The grant of New Netherlands to the duke of York (Ibid., p. 136) reserved a rent of forty beaver skins, if demanded. The grant of Pennsylvania to William Penn speaks of the Castle of Windsor and reserves two beaver skins and a fifth of the gold and silver ore (Ibid., p. 185). Georgia was holden as of the honour of Hampton Court in the county of Middlesex at a rent of four shillings for every hundred acres that should be settled (Ibid., p. 242).

The tenure of Bombay.

69. Charter of 1669 printed among Charters granted to the East India Company (no date or publisher's name): 'to be holden of us, our heirs and successors as of the manor of East Greenwich in the county of Kent, in free and common soccage and not in capite nor by knight's service, yielding and paying therefor to us, our heirs and successors at the Custom House, London, the rent or sum of ten pounds of lawful money of England in gold on the thirtieth day of September yearly for ever.'

The tenure of Prince Rupert's land.

70. Charter of 1670 incorporating the Hudson's Bay Company, printed by Beckles Wilson, The Great Company, vol. II., pp. 318, 327: 'yielding and paying yearly to us…two elks and two black beavers, whensoever and as often as we our heirs and successors shall happen to enter into the said countries, territories and regions hereby granted.'

Kent and Blackstone.

71. Thayer, The Teaching of English Law at Universities in Harvard Law Review, vol. IX., p. 170: '"I retired to a country village," Chancellor Kent tells us in speaking of the breaking up of Yale College by the war, where he was a student in 1779, "and, finding Blackstone's Commentaries, I read the four volumes…The work inspired me at the age of fifteen with awe, and I fondly determined to be a lawyer."…"There is abundant evidence," if we may rely upon the authority of Dr Hammond, whose language I quote, "of the immediate absorption of nearly twenty-five hundred copies of the Commentaries in the thirteen colonies before the Declaration of Independence." '

Marshall and Blackstone.

72. Thayer, John Marshall, 1901, p. 6: 'When Marshall was about eighteen years old he began to study Blackstone…He seems to have found a copy of Blackstone in his father's house…Just now the first American edition was out (Philadelphia, 1771—2), in which the list of subscribers, headed by the name of "John Adams, barrister at law, Boston," had also that of "Captain Thomas Marshall, Clerk of Dunmore County."'

Roman law in America.

73. It may be interesting to notice that in 1856, and perhaps even in 1871, Sir H. Maine believed that the Code of Louisiana ('of all republications of Roman law the one which appears to us the clearest, the fullest, the most

philosophical and the best adapted to the exigencies of modern society ') had a grand destiny before it in the United States. 'Now it is this code, and not the Common Law of England which the newest American States are taking for the substratum of their laws...The Roman law is, therefore, fast becoming the lingua franca of universal jurisprudence.' (Maine, Roman Law and Legal Education, 1856, reprinted in Village Communities, ed. 3, pp. 360 I.) Nowadays this hope or fear of a Reception of Roman law in the United States seems, so I am given to understand, quite unfounded. See e.g. J. F. Dillon, Laws and Jurisprudence of England and America, 1894, p. 155: 'the common law is the basis of the laws of every State and Territory of the Union, with comparatively unimportant and gradually waning exceptions.'
Ihering and the litigious English man.
74. Ihering, Der Kampf um's Recht, ed. 10, pp. 45, 69: 'Ich habe bereits oben das Beispiel des kampflustigen Engländers angeführt, und ich kann hier nur wiederholen, was ich dort gesagt: in dem Gulden, um den er hartnäckig streitet, steckt die politische Entwicklung Englands. Einem Volke, bei dem es allgemeine Uebung ist, dass Jeder auch im Kleinen und Kleinsten sein Recht tapfer behauptet, wird Niemand wagen, das Höchste, was es hat, zu entreissen, und es ist daher kein Zufall, dass dasselbe Volk des Alterthums, welches im Innern die höchste politische Entwicklung und nach Aussen hin die grösste Kraftentfaltung aufzuweisen hat, das römische, zugleich das ausgebildetste Privatrecht besass.'
Codes in English Colonies.
75. Thus in particular Queensland in 1899 enacted a criminal code of 707 sections. See Journal of the Society of Comparative Legislation, New Ser., vol. VI., pp. 555 560: 'The precedents utilised in framing the Code were the draft English codes of 1879 and '880, the Italian Penal Code of 1888, and the Penal Code of the State of New York.' See also Ilbert, Legislative Methods, p. 155.
The German Civil Code.
76. Some information in English about the new German code will be found in articles by Mr E. Schuster, Law Quarterly Review, vol. XII., p. 17, and Journal of the Society of Comparative Legislation, Old Series, vol. I., p. 191. Despite the careful exclusion of almost all words derived from the Latin (except Hypothek, which happens to be Greek), the new law book may look Roman to an Englishman; but then it does not look Roman to Germans. The following sentences are taken from a speech delivered in the Reichstag (Mugdan, Materialien zum bürgerlichen Gesetzbuch, vol. I., pp. 876—7): 'In dieser Beziehung ist vor Allem der Vorwurf gegen den Entwurf erhoben, er enthalte materiell kein deutsches Recht...Selten ist ein Vorwurf unbegründeter gewesen...Das Sachenrecht ist von A bis Z durchaus deutsches Recht...Was dann den Begriff des Besitzes betrifft, von der ganzen römischen Besitztheorie ist nichts übrig geblieben...Der

allgemeine Theil des Obligationenrechtes ist natürlich römischen Ursprunges...Kommen wir aber zu den einzelnen speziellen Rechtsgeschäften, so treffen wir auch da sofort wieder deutsches Recht...Auch das Familienrecht ist durchaus deutschrechtlich...Dann ist das Erbrecht durch und durch deutschrechtlichen Ursprunges...' The supposition that codification means romanization is baseless; it may mean deromanization. But the great lesson to be learnt by Englishmen from the German Code is that a democratically elected assembly, which is for many purposes divided into bitterly contending fractions, can be induced to show a wonderful forbearance when uniformity of law is to be attained.

Unity of law.

77. Molinaeus (Charles Du Moulin), Oratio de concordia et unione consuetudinum Franciae, in Opera (1681), vol. II., p. 691: 'Mihi quoque videtur nihil aptius, nihil efficacius ad plures provincias sub eodem imperio retinendas et fovendas, nee fortius nee honestius vinculum quam communio et conformitas eorundem morum legumve utilium et aequabilium.'

The school at Harvard.

78. The name of Harvard is here mentioned without prejudice to the just claims of any other American university; but the Harvard Law Review, edited by a committee of students, is a journal of which any school might be proud.